Reading Improvement

in the Elementary School

Reading Improvement
in the Elementary School —

DONALD C. CUSHENBERY

Parker Publishing Company, Inc.   **West Nyack, N.Y.**

A WORD FROM THE AUTHOR ABOUT THIS BOOK . . .

I was inspired to compile this volume because large numbers of experienced teachers in my classes, workshops, and institutes in many different states have often voiced the need for a professional book which is not voluminous and yet is practical. This material is intended for the many other in-service teachers whom I have good reason to feel have similar beliefs. The work is a synthesis of practical suggestions I have gained from nearly twenty-five years of experience as a teacher and researcher of reading at all educational levels as well as knowledge gained from reading many volumes on the subject.

My chief concerns have been to present useful suggestions for the classroom teacher; to include straightforward, pointed discussions which would lend insights into various reading concepts; and to provide the reader with data concerning available books, materials, and other aids. Appropriate selected references have been included at the close of each chapter for those readers who have special need for a more amplified discussion of certain topics.

Chapter 1 contains a discussion of the products of the reading act and the principles of effective reading instruction. The first stage of reading instruction, reading readiness, is reviewed in Chapter 2. In Chapter 3 a complete survey of the primary reading program is developed, including suggestions for oral, silent, functional, and recreatory reading instruction. The objectives and the nature of the intermediate and upper grade reading curriculum are presented in Chapter 4.

The heart of the reading act, word perception, with all of its major facets, is emphasized in Chapter 5. In Chapter 6, the teacher's role in building effective comprehension skills, the end product of the reading act, is developed. Practical suggestions for helping each child with content area reading skills are included in Chapter 7.

Of interest to many reading educators is a terse discussion in Chapter 8 of the pros and cons concerning the many current approaches to the teaching of reading at all levels of the instructional program. The purposes, factors, and principles to be observed in the use of evaluation instruments are surveyed in Chapter 9. A very brief presentation is made in Chapter 10 of the role of the elementary teacher in federally funded reading programs.

The appendixes have been chosen with care in order to satisfy the many requests which I have received for this kind of information. No attempt has been made to list prices or fees since this information is subject to frequent change. The reader should consult the latest catalogues of the various companies for cost information. Restrictions have not been placed on the number and kinds of materials listed; therefore, each school official will need to be selective in terms of interest and financial resources. The listing of a material at any point in the volume does not necessarily imply endorsement on the part of the author.

The selection of chapter topics was undertaken with much thought and deliberation in order to present only those subjects which would be of significant interest to the classroom teacher. To accomplish this goal, numerous teachers who have assignments in all types of socio-economic neighborhoods were surveyed formally and informally regarding aspects of reading instruction which should be discussed. The final selection of topics was based on the results of these studies.

Donald C. Cushenbery

ACKNOWLEDGMENTS

Grateful appreciation is extended to my fellow reading educators, to the many classroom teachers who have been students in my various graduate classes, and to Dr. A. Sterl Artley, my doctoral advisor and friend, for providing the necessary stimulation and encouragement which led to the eventual publication of this book. I also wish to extend thanks to Dr. Donavon Lumpkin of Ball State University and Mr. Mike Currier, my graduate assistant, for their aid in the development of several of the appendixes.

I am indebted to Mr. Ronald Meyer, Director of The Central Reading Clinic, Omaha Public Schools; and Mr. Michael Ward, University of Nebraska at Omaha. Various companies as well as several reading authorities have allowed me to reprint several pieces of information. Appropriate recognition is given at numerous locations in the book for this permission.

CONTENTS

APPENDIXES

Reading Improvement
in the Elementary School

1

Analyzing Key Factors in Reading

Throughout recorded history man has grappled with what seems to be a very simple question, "What is reading?" Reading is more than "talk written down." We know it is not a simple act of just pronouncing words.

Reading is the complex act of recognizing visual symbols and interpreting these symbols in terms of the reader's background of experiences. In order for pupils to gain the maximum benefit from the school's reading program, a number of principles for the teaching of reading should be kept in mind by the total faculty. Teaching a child to read effectively has been, and continues to be, one of the most important objectives of the educational curriculum. When pupils leave the high school, teachers should be able to say that the students are competent in such areas as word perception, comprehension, and study skills.

In the various sections which follow, a discussion of a number of significant topics which relate to the facets mentioned in the previous paragraph is provided. Particular attention has been given to the reading tasks, the products of the reading act, principles of effective reading instruction, the place of reading in the general curriculum, the objectives of the elementary school reading program, and the specific goals of reading instruction. A summary of the total discussion is included at the close of the chapter.

The Reading Tasks

The first task in reading is that of word perception. A child can never gain the ideas and moods of the writer if he cannot recognize the words. How does the twentieth-century child learn to pronounce words?

Each pupil at every level must be provided with a variety of techniques for attacking different kinds of words. In some instances, he may find a phonetic generalization which will suit his exact needs. On other occasions, he may try to master a word by taking it apart and studying the separate components of prefixes, root words, and suffixes.

At other times, a picture or context clue may be of greatest help to him—or it is entirely possible (in fact, quite probable) that he will make use of a combination of these tools to serve his purpose.

However, reading is much more than just the mouthing of words from a page. Words mean nothing unless they convey the desired message to students. A rich background of experiences is important at this stage and the contributions of both the teacher and the parents are very critical. Teachers who provide rich and meaningful reading readiness activities are aiding the cause of better reading comprehension. The parent who takes his child to the zoo and lets him *see* an elephant is building a background of understanding for his child when the child sees the word, E-L-E-P-H-A-N-T, in print. A child who has never seen an elephant or the picture of one could hardly have the correct conception of what the word means when he sees it in a story about jungle animals.

Reading does not stop with word recognition and comprehension. Advertisers would find that newspaper and magazine ads would be a sheer waste of money if that were the case. The ad writer or journalist would hope that the reader would react favorably to what he has read. Politicians, religious leaders, and philosophers have this aspect in mind when they write and distribute materials to candidates for membership in their respective causes. It is vitally important that pupils REACT to what they have read in accordance with their own experiences. This point is illustrated by the story of a precocious American child who was visiting his cousin in an elementary school in Germany. An excited child dashed into the room and wrote the German word for "FIRE" on the greenboard. The teacher and children left the room as quickly as possible. The puzzled guest could pronounce the word, but since he had no background of experience with regard to it, he could not understand the actions of those present.

Successful achievement in reading results in a number of wholesome outcomes or products for the pupil. These aspects are described in the section which follows in order that the teacher might help determine if pupils' reading skills are at satisfactory levels.

The Products of the Reading Act

If the reading act is completed properly, the child should grasp the meaning and intentions which the writer intended to convey. Reading is a two-way process of communication between the writer and the reader. When a pupil reads, he interprets a selection in terms of his own experiences. For example, Robert Frost's, *On Stopping by the Woods on a Snowy Evening,* would no doubt have a much different meaning for a child who has always lived in Vermont than for the boy or girl who has always lived on a desert. A child can be helped to grasp the writer's feelings by the use of pictures and other audio-visual aids.

The development of various reading rates is an important outcome of effective reading instruction. Reading for details when a student is preparing for a comprehensive examination calls for a slow, deliberate reading; however, reading for main ideas from a newspaper can be accomplished by the skimming method at a high rate of speed. The teacher is a key factor in the development of various kinds of reading purposes. One might well ask a class: "Read the following page to find out why Uncle Frank was angry with Billy." This approach lends help in developing a reason or purpose for reading. If one merely says, "Read pages 20 to 27 in your reader," without further direction, he is really contributing to ineffective comprehension.

One of the leading outcomes of effective reading is the desire to want to read widely for many purposes. Skills and competencies are vital, but these aspects are only means toward the end. Unless the child applies his reading skills to gain clearer understandings, to perceive social and historical relationships, and to develop permanent interests in reading, it might well be that the reading objectives of a given school need closer inspection.

Developing critical readers should be an important product of any reading program. Pupils should be able to differentiate between a fact and an opinion as early as the third or fourth grade and, indeed, should be taught how to do this through direct, sequential instructional techniques. Ability to read critically has always been a characteristic of an able reader. Today, perhaps more than ever before, a pupil needs to check carefully what he reads against a reputable source. The child or adult who believes what he reads in a book or text is true can be lead to believe some ridiculous statements.

The pupil must be encouraged to look for evidence to support beliefs about a certain situation. If he has been taught to check references, the writer's capabilities, and other factors, he soon learns to withhold judgment until he can find a suitable basis for his ideas.

All of the commendable outgrowths which accrue for the pupils in a given school have come about because teachers have subscribed to certain principles of reading instruction. The most significant of these principles are discussed in the next section.

PRINCIPLES OF EFFECTIVE READING INSTRUCTION

1. *Effective reading instruction is based on the individual needs of each pupil.* Grouping of children into small groups within the classroom or by any one of at least twenty other known grouping methods serves to narrow the ability ranges found in any one group; however, unless one makes a serious attempt to evaluate the strengths and limitations of each child and

helps the child in light of this knowledge, lasting success in reading is never really accomplished. For many, many years a sizable amount of "lip service" has been given to the idea that "we take the child where we find him," but the actual practice with respect to this axiom is less than encouraging—in fact, a few teachers in the middle and upper grades appear to believe that even the assignment of pupils into small working groups for particular reading assignments and lessons is not necessary.

2. *Proper instruction in reading for individual children is based on a thorough analysis of each pupil's strengths and limitations in the basic reading skill areas.* In a typical heterogeneous fourth grade class, children can be found who are reading at any stage from second through seventh grade levels, for sixth grade pupils as many as eight levels may be found, and for eighth grade pupils as many as ten levels may be found. Any individual child may display satisfactory performance in one or more areas of the reading skills and perform at an unsatisfactory level with regard to other skills. The establishment of programs and procedures for meeting the individual reading needs of pupils is obviously very important at all grade levels.

In order to design a program which will be of maximum aid to a pupil or group of pupils, one must have explicit information regarding the current status of the reading competencies of each pupil. The diagnosis can be accomplished through the use of teacher-made tests, informal inventories, standardized tests, and the teacher's astute observation. Proper diagnosis can serve as a warning before undesirable habits and unhealthy emotional conditions impede a potentially capable pupil. A survey test may serve the purpose of being a rough screening device for dividing pupils in the higher, middle, and lower reading groups; however, it tells little about the individual needs of children. For those children in the lower reading groups, an individual analysis is very desirable. Time must be taken to use a subjective reading inventory, or a commercial instrument such as the *Durrell Analysis of Reading Difficulty* or the *Diagnostic Reading Scales.* (These and other instruments are described in the chapter on evaluation.) These measures indicate a subject's ability in such areas as sight words, oral reading, and word attack skills. One should take the information derived from these instruments, make a checklist of the areas of limitation, and provide appropriate lessons which will serve to overcome these deficiencies. One of the most important factors to be determined is that of the instructional level of each child; this author has discovered in his reading clinic that all too many of the clients have been forced to read from materials which are considerably above their instructional levels. Frustration and discouragement have been the result for these children.

The subjective reading inventory is easily constructed. The first step is to select a story of moderate length from each basal reader from the pre-primer through the eighth grade levels of a series which has not been read by the student. The child should read the first two-thirds of a given story silently. He should then take a comprehension test which the teacher has previously constructed. If the subject scores above 90 per cent on the test, one might assume that that particular level is the child's independent reading level; from 75 to 89 per cent, his instructional level; and 74 per cent and below, his frustration level. The last third of the story should be read orally with notations made for each omission, substitution, repetition, or addition. If the child pronounces from 98 to 100 per cent of the words correctly, one might assume that his oral reading efficiency is at an independent level; from 95 to 97 per cent, his instructional level; and 94 per cent and below, his frustration level. Even though there is some question about the authenticity of the true grade levels of various basal readers, the subjective inventory represents a reasonably accurate measure of the child's instructional level.

3. *The teacher must use a variety of approaches with different children.* Nearly every method and procedure which has been described in the literature is reported by various researchers to have been successful with some children at some time. A single, rigid mind-set should not be developed with respect to any given set of materials. Leading reading authorities have pointed out for many years that all materials have advantages and limitations and that no one aid is so superior to all others that it should be used to the exclusion of all other teaching devices. There appears to be ample evidence that some children will learn to read successfully, despite the method or approach used by a given teacher; however, a number of disabled readers are also in evidence in nearly all programs. Because different children have different needs, a variety of approaches and materials should be used to meet the various limitations of pupils. The vast array of materials now being sold should be treated very much the same way that a physician treats drugs in a pharmacy. The teacher's job is to write a "prescription" for each child and select those materials which appear to best suit his needs.

4. *The concept of reading readiness must be made a part of the reading program at all educational levels.* Even though educators commonly think of "reading readiness" as being associated almost entirely with teaching children at the first grade level, the importance of its requirement must be stressed at all levels.

When pupils are forced to read materials in advance of their levels of experiential background, they very often develop wide differences in meaning for various words. These children tend to mouth the words without any clear concept of their meanings. The principle of readiness for learning means that experiences will not be forced on any child at any age if the stage of the child's development is not adequate. Readiness is a condition indicating that the child is ready to engage in different reading experiences at various academic levels without noticeable physical or emotional discomfort.

The appearance of readiness for any type of learning for any particular individual is governed by a number of factors: physical, mental, emotional, and social. However, time cannot be wasted for the proper stage of readiness to occur. The wise teacher at any level will provide a broad range of experiences which will serve to sharpen the pupil's general interest in reading.

The readiness concept must be dealt with in the learning situation at the high school and college levels. Teachers who ignore the principles relating to readiness assign materials to be read which are much beyond the experiential backgrounds of the readers—and this leads to utter discouragement and disinterest in the entire educational program at those levels. Knowing when to introduce certain learning and reading experiences is a matter of astute judgment. Careful observation will help to determine if sufficient readiness has been established for a particular educational experience.

5. *The reading program at the elementary level should be geared to prevent reading problems instead of undue emphasis on "cure" techniques.* Educators should not be proud to have to admit that massive "crash" programs in remedial reading are seemingly necessary at the intermediate, junior high, and senior high levels. Hundreds of schools at this very moment have either planned programs or are planning programs, using funds from the Elementary and Secondary Education Act, for the sole purpose of attempting to upgrade the reading skills of thousands of pupils. There are a few children for which it will be virtually impossible to bring up to grade level in reading and this fact might as well be accepted.

Educators should be concerned about strengthening each teacher's abilities in the principles and procedures of effective reading instruction and thus help to prevent the need for remedial programs. The early detection of possible reading deficiencies and the provision of help at an early date to overcome the limitations are important characteristics of an effective reading program. Even after these principles have been followed and pupils have become proficient readers, one must be able to perceive the relationship of competency in reading to all other facets of the curriculum. The next topic contains a discussion relating to this concept.

THE PLACE OF READING IN THE GENERAL CURRICULUM

Millions of students are enrolled in the elementary and secondary schools throughout the nation, seeking an education that will equip them to compete with other citizens of the society for jobs and other opportunities.

With the creation of the jet age, increasing demands are being made to train the youth of today to become leaders in a complex society. At no time in the history of our country has there been greater emphasis placed upon academic training as the important factor in obtaining a position. The critical eyes of many people are focused on the school systems to determine the value of the curriculum for meeting the needs of today's youth.

To the informed public, learning to be effective in reading all kinds of material is of utmost importance. Many ideas can be advanced for this heightened concern about the quality of reading instruction. At the outset, there is the status concept: The elementary pupil or adult who reads poorly tends to lack the approval of his peers. Second, reading is a vital instrument by which children acquire information in arithmetic, social studies, and other subjects at every educational level. Third, every citizen is required in varying degrees to read books and documents if he is to be an informed person with regard to current events. Beginning at approximately the fourth grade, the elementary child is asked to read in many different subject areas in addition to the familiar materials found in a basal reader or trade book. Frequently, little individual attention is given to individual pupils while they are trying to cope with subject area material. To be successful in his work, the child must necessarily develop independence in his study habits.

It is unfortunate that many children, and even adults, achieve satisfactory success in reading library volumes, but fail miserably in the subject areas because they have not developed adequate comprehension skills. Many times they fail to set a purpose for reading and are unable to scan and skim given material properly in light of a given purpose.

Each content area, if it is to be mastered by the reader, must be read only after the reader has acquired a general body of study skills. It is not at all uncommon to find that many classroom assignments in the intermediate and upper grades are either ignored or misinterpreted because the child has the feeling that he has little clear understanding of what to do or how to do it. The teacher can do much to help the child acquire suitable reading skills for the various content areas. A complete discussion of the relationship of reading to each of the content areas is explained in Chapter 7.

In order to bring together all of the previous topics into a proper focus, an outline of the specific goals of reading instruction is provided in the next section. Check the goals of the present reading program against those that have been indicated.

SPECIFIC GOALS OF READING INSTRUCTION

One must realize that there are a number of objectives which might be produced for each of the various phases of reading instruction. Some goals

are the specific province of the elementary teacher, others of the intermediate teacher, and still others of the upper grade teacher. The adminis-
trative official who is in charge of the total program must see the reading
curriculum from kindergarten through the university levels. Each teacher in
a particular school system must see his or her role as an educational agent
making a substantial contribution toward the total set of goals.

1. One of the major goals of an effective reading program is that of the
   development of independence in word recognition. The instructional
   program should provide the child with a series of sequential lessons
   in the following areas:

   A. Recognizing whole words by sight
   B. Analyzing words through the use of phonetic generalizations
   C. Using context clues
   D. Using the tools of structural analysis
   E. Employing the use of the dictionary

2. Since it is necessary to gain different types of understanding from the
   printed page, the pupil needs to build and maintain adequate skills in
   the area of comprehension. Such areas would include:

   A. Learning to follow directions
   B. Constructing outlines and summaries
   C. Learning to perceive the order of events and ideas
   D. Reading to find the main idea
   E. Reading to select specific significant details
   F. Differentiating between fact and opinion
   G. Developing ability to predict outcomes and anticipate events
   H. Developing ability to arrive at conclusions and generalizations
      from a particular reading selection
   I. Developing skills in reading maps, graphs, and charts
   J. Refining ability in getting meaning from phrases, sentences, para-
      graphs, and stories (in that order)
   K. Analyzing cause and effect relationships

3. Because the child needs to become adept with respect to the different
   study skills, it is necessary that he receive training throughout the
   reading program in the following areas:

   A. Using the table of contents
   B. Using the different types of dictionaries and the glossaries found
      in various basal readers and context area books
   C. Understanding the use of the index
   D. Employing the use of specialized sources such as encyclopedias,
      World Almanac, and other materials
   E. Locating key words
   F. Organizing, writing, and reporting significant information
   G. Using non-reference books
   H. Interpreting various punctuation marks, diacritical marks, sym-
      bols, and abbreviations which are unique to a particular volume

4. The total school program must cultivate a genuine, lasting desire to read on the part of every child in the instructional program. To achieve this goal, the reading curriculum should provide for:

   A. Ample amount of time for free reading in books which are on both the interest and ability levels of the children
   B. Dramatizations of stories for a single class or the total school population
   C. Discussions of various books by individuals or groups
   D. Oral presentations of various parts of books
   E. Book exhibits to serve as "interest getters"
   F. Integration of book selections with other classroom units
   G. Art activities which portray various scenes from books
   H. Brief book reports which serve as "teasers" for the rest of a group

As the child progresses through the total reading curriculum, he should be given instruction and opportunities which will result in the realization of the goals previously described. The job of adapting the curriculum to the needs of given children is possible, and a dedicated teacher who is instilled with the objectives of a vital, on-going reading program such as has been described in this chapter is the most important ingredient in seeing that this task is accomplished.

Summary

Learning to be an effective reader is not a simple task. Reading is a complex act consisting of word perception, comprehension, and reaction. A child who is enrolled in a reading program which is designed to meet his individual needs can expect to receive several benefits, including the interpretation of the writer's ideas and feelings, the development of various reading rates, the construction of critical reading skills, and the improvement of personal growth.

A successful reading program is realized only after all teachers are committed to following the specific principles of effective reading instruction which have been discussed in this chapter. Reading is the key to success in all content areas and thus might well be one of the most important areas of competency to be developed during a child's lifetime.

All teachers in the elementary school should see their responsibilities as a part of the total set of reading goals to be achieved by every child in a given school system.

Selected References

1. Bond, Guy L. and Wagner, Eva Bond. *Teaching the Child to Read.* (Fourth Edition) New York: The Macmillan Company, 1966, Chapters 3 and 4.
2. DeBoer, John J. and Dallman, Martha. *The Teaching of Reading.* (Re-

vised Edition) New York: Holt, Rinehart and Winston, Inc., 1964, Chapter 1.

3. Dechant, Emerald V. *Improving the Teaching of Reading.* Englewood Cliffs, N.J.: Prentice-Hall, Inc., 1964, Chapter 2.

4. Heilman, Arthur W. *Principles and Practices of Teaching Reading.* (Second Edition) Columbus: Charles E. Merrill Books, Inc., 1967, Chapter 2.

5. McKee, Paul. *Reading: A Program of Instruction for the Elementary School.* Boston: Houghton Mifflin Company, 1966, Chapters 1 and 2.

6. Russell, David H. *Children Learn to Read.* (Second Edition) Boston: Ginn and Company, 1961, Chapters 1 and 2.

7. Schubert, Delwyn G. and Torgerson, Theodore L. (Editors). *Readings in Reading: Practice Theory Research.* New York: Thomas Y. Crowell Company, 1968, Section 1.

8. Smith, Henry P. and Dechant, Emerald V. *Psychology in Teaching Reading.* Englewood Cliffs, N.J.: Prentice-Hall, Inc., 1961, Chapter 1.

9. Smith, Nila B. *Reading Instruction for Today's Children.* Englewood Cliffs, N.J.: Prentice-Hall, Inc., 1963, Chapters 1 and 2.

2

Preparing for the Reading Readiness Period

Guiding every young child to that stage in his educational program when he is ready for formal reading instruction is one of the most important jobs of a primary teacher. In order to accomplish this task one must understand the definition of reading readiness; the relationship of such aspects as social development, mental abilities, background of experience, physical development, and language development to reading readiness; the methods and techniques for strengthening various readiness areas; and the nature and kinds of appraisal tools for determining each child's abilities in this important area. This chapter contains a frank, practical discussion of these important topics.

The Definition of Reading Readiness

The term, "reading readiness," suggests that a child has reached a level in his educational growth when he is able to read without obvious discomforts of a physical, psychological, or emotional nature. Actually readiness is an important element at all stages of reading growth, from the early primary grade years through adulthood. The children in every classroom are always moving toward another "rung" in the reading "ladder" of skills. To gain proficiency in reading, each pupil must have adequate readiness for each succeeding level of understanding.

Reading readiness as applied to very young children might be called "beginning reading readiness," whereas readiness as related to later reading stages might be referred to as "specific reading readiness." This chapter is concerned with the former term.

To get a child to the level of beginning reading readiness makes some rather demanding requirements on the part of both parents and teachers. The development of general mental, emotional, and physical preparedness for reading requires understanding and attentive parents coupled with perceptive teachers who are thoroughly familiar with the entire process of learning to read. Nearly all children are eager to read. The teacher has the responsibility of working closely with the parents in steering the child to the place and time when eagerness to read makes the transition to the actual reading act.

THE RELATIONSHIP OF CERTAIN FACTORS AND READINESS TO READ

The direct responsibility for determining when each pupil is ready to read is contingent upon several factors. In making this decision, one should take into consideration a number of very important factors such as social development, mental capacity, background of experience, physical characteristics (such as the ability to make auditory and visual discriminations), and general language development. These factors and their relationship to the reading act are discussed in the following section.

Social Development

One of the most difficult tasks for the young pupil is that of working with other children in a school situation. The class is an organized group in which each child is expected to interact successfully with the other members of the class. The understanding and general approach used by educators will determine to a large extent the degree of success which any one pupil can obtain in group relations with his peers.

The child's success with the reading act is positively related to the manner in which he is accepted socially. Before coming to school, each pupil has been the center of attention in the family group and has had little responsibility for working actively with others on a joint project or activity. The success of the reading program with small working groups demands that each child be reliant and cooperative in the social situation.

Successful progression of the total reading program calls for a myriad of activities which place pupils together in cooperative endeavors. A child who is deficient in any of the areas suggested by the questions listed later in this chapter will be at a disadvantage in learning to read. Careful guidance will help pupils to share with others, to work with other children in the group, and to consider the rights of others. An analysis of the strengths and limitations of each pupil in this important area will help to designate which pupils need direct help in the various areas.

Mental Abilities

As this volume is being prepared, authorities are in disagreement regarding the minimum mental age which should be attained before a child begins formal reading experiences. For many years, the figure most often quoted by speakers and writers has been that of six years and six months. The results of the Morphett-Washburn study of 1931 indicated that those children in the study who had mental ages of less than six years, six months showed little success in reading achievement.[9]

In recent years, a number of investigations have appeared to suggest that, even though there is a high degree of relationship between mental age and ease of learning to read, this factor is by no means the most important factor to be considered. Sister Nila's study in 1953 concluded that the four factors related to reading readiness in order of importance were (1) auditory discrimination, (2) visual discrimination, (3) range of information, and (4) mental age.[10]

The importance of mental age should not be minimized. A mental age of at least six would seem to be necessary, since a child with this characteristic is apt to have an acceptable span of attention and to be observant with respect to those factors in his environment which will further aid his general knowledge.

The question of how to work with those children with less than desirable mental age levels presents a number of problems for the primary teacher. These children, of course, need much individual attention. They will need to be placed in the reading program at a much slower rate than the children with higher levels. Some will need numerous language experiences of both the formal and incidental types. Activities which might be suitable for this group are described later.

Background of Experience

One of the most important ingredients in shaping successful readers is that of background of experience. A word has meaning to a child only if he has had some experience with the real and/or imaginary aspects which make up the meaning of the word. Reading is the recognition of visual symbols in light of the background of experiences of the reader. A child who is confronted with the word, "apple," might be able to pronounce the word from any one or more of the word attack techniques; however, if he has never *seen* an apple, *smelled* an apple or *eaten* an apple, it is quite doubtful that he will have the proper interpretation of what the word really means.

A child who has had a wide background of experience is in a much better position to talk, to read, and to write about pictures and words. He is better able to understand simple stories in the pre-primers and primers because he has had direct experience with many persons and objects. Provisions must be made for those children who have had limited experiences.

What two basic implications can be derived in view of the previous information? First, one must observe each child carefully with respect to the magnitude and depth of his experiences. This can be done through the use of anecdotal records and through careful listening to the everyday language patterns of the children. Second, if deficiencies are noted, plans must be made to reinforce the pupil's understanding of various words through the use of field trips, audio-visual aids, explanations, and demonstrations. (Details of some of these techniques are described later in the chapter.)

Physical Characteristics

Every child entering the first grade is given a complete physical examination in most school systems of America. This practice is very desirable, since there are several physical defects such as poor vision and substandard hearing which can have a significant effect on a given child's success in reading. A high level of auditory and visual discrimination, as suggested by Sister Nila's study, is one of the most important requirements for learning to read. The handicaps of inadequate sight or hearing are all too obvious.

If a medical screening is not possible, observation should be undertaken for indications which may suggest that physical anomalies might be present. The pupil who rubs his eyes may be in dire need of glasses. If a child pays little or no attention to specific directions, one might well suspect a hearing defect rather than inadequate intelligence. These children should be referred immediately to the local or county health nurse for further investigation and referrals made if necessary. Many local service clubs such as Lions and Kiwanis have funds available for needy families for such items as glasses, hearing aids, and professional services.

In recent years, there has been much discussion about the role of lateral dominance and reading ability. While a large number of research studies have recently been concerned with this aspect, there is little concrete evidence to show that variations in eye, foot, or hand dominance have any significant relationship to reading readiness. Importance should be attached to those factors which have unquestioned importance.

Language Development

The typical first grade child is able to speak in sentences and has several thousand words in his speaking vocabulary. However, a few pupils can always be detected who use short sentences which are fragmented and incorrectly phrased. These pupils have perhaps lived in a deprived home environment in which the members of the family speak in short sentences and make use of few words.

The mastery of spoken language is important for a high level of success in reading. A pupil's store of words will determine to a large degree his ability to communicate and understand many different concepts. His everyday conversation will also reveal the nature of his knowledge of sentence structure. Enriched reading experiences are predicated upon the pupil's ability to demonstrate a wide variety of spoken words.

Language development can be accelerated through the use of pictures, demonstrations, audio-visual aids, and carefully devised questioning techniques. Certain commercial materials such as the *Language Experience Kit A* (Ginn), the *Peabody Language Development Kit* (American Guidance), and the *Listen-Hear* and *Junior Listen-Hear Books* (Follett) have also been used with success by some teachers in aiding language growth. A new program, *TRY* (Noble and Noble, Publishers), which develops visual-motor skills and oral language, is now on the market and is being used in some schools. The *EFI Reading Readiness Program* (Electronic Futures, Inc.) is structured into modules to enable individualization of reading readiness lessons for individual students or groups of students. These materials have been constructed to allow for the presentation of a series of language development lessons in sequence. Appropriate manuals and guidebooks contain many suggestions for the teacher.

RECOMMENDATIONS FOR STRENGTHENING READINESS TO READ

The resourceful, imaginative teacher should not depend solely on commercial materials. There is a significant place for creative planning to meet the needs of given pupils in a given school.

In the section which follows, a number of activities and suggestions have been included which will serve to elevate the child's reading readiness level in those areas which deal with auditory and visual discrimination; physical handicaps; experience, language, and cultural deprivation; and social and/ or emotional handicaps.

Suggestions for Aiding Auditory and Visual Discrimination

The development of auditory and visual discrimination is one of the most important facets of the readiness program. The child must be able to differentiate between sounds of words and letters and have the ability to see the differences between written words and letters. The following is a brief description of a few approaches which might be used to develop suitable ability in this area.

1. The teacher pronounces a group of words with the same beginning sound. The pupils are asked to mention other words with the same sounds. A poster with several pictures can be displayed and each child is asked to point to a picture which would represent a word with the same sound stressed earlier in the exercise.

2. The teacher presents an exercise involving the use of a series of squares with each square containing four words. Each child is asked to draw a line between the two (or three) words which are the same. The exercise can be varied by having three words which are the same and one word which is different in each box. The pupil is directed to draw a circle around the word which is different.

3. Another exercise similar to the one above involves the use of two lists of words on a page. The boys and girls are requested to draw lines between words which look the same.

4. A simple word such as "sat" is pronounced. The children are asked to find the picture of an object on a particular page which rhymes with "sat."

5. A page with the picture of a man and woman is placed on the child's desk. Numerous items of clothing are located at the side of the page. The pupil is asked to draw a line from the man or woman to the item of clothing that the particular person is wearing.

6. Several common words are pronounced which are within the meaning vocabulary of the boys and girls. Each child is to put an "X" on the picture on the page which represents the word pronounced. (The pictures are placed in random order.)

7. A page is presented which has a series of five pictures in each of several rows. The teacher names all of the objects in any given row. She asks each pupil to mark the object which has the same beginning sound as the first object in the row.

8. Large pictures can be pasted on cardboard sheets and then cut into smaller pieces. The child is asked to re-arrange the pieces to form a picture. Commercial puzzles which are suitable for young children can also be employed.

9. A large picture which has many colors and objects is shown. Each pupil is asked to name as many different objects as he can find in the picture. The same direction is given with respect to the different colors.

10. Read very simple poems and ask the children to name words which rhyme with a stimulus word which has been mentioned before the exercise. Each should raise his hand when he hears a rhyming word.

Provisions for Aiding Physical Handicaps

1. As mentioned earlier in this chapter, all children should receive a screening examination by the school nurse or school doctor for any physical problems which might be present. If results of these examinations indicate suspected physical abnormalities, the teacher should recommend a thorough medical examination to the parent.

2. Frequent rest periods should be given to those children who appear to be frail. Learn as much as possible about each pupil's physical condition and construct lesson plans in terms of complexity and length in light of this information. Too many teachers are guilty of making plans for the group and expecting each child to conform.

3. Conferences should be conducted with each parent in order to learn as much as possible about each pupil's eating and sleeping patterns. If undue tiredness is obvious, tactful suggestions with regard to additional sleep should be made to the parent.

4. Attention should be given to the location of each child's desk or seat. Those students who display poor vision or poor hearing should be located near the teacher and near the area where materials are being presented.

5. The visual approach should be used with those who are hard-of-hearing. The use of pointers may be employed to emphasize certain features of a given chart or picture.

6. For those pupils who display poor muscular coordination, the use of a large number of rhythmical games which make use of the feet, hands, and head are particularly appropriate. These should be accompanied by music from a piano or record player when conditions permit. The formation of a rhythm band is also an important aid in improving coordination.

7. Many commercial games which are manipulative in nature are available to the teacher. Those which employ the use of pegboards and formboards are particularly suitable.

Recommendations for Helping Those with Experience, Language, and Cultural Deprivation

1. These children need a series of experiences such as field trips to places in the community—different kinds of stores, the fire station, the zoo, a local farm, or even to all areas of the school building itself. Following the trips, a careful development of new words and concepts should be undertaken. They should be encouraged to draw pictures and to talk about the experiences relating to the various trips. There is no substitute for direct contacts of this type for

enriching vocabulary and making each child aware of his surroundings.

2. If extensive field trips cannot be undertaken, the use of appropriate films and filmstrips relating to the community and the community helpers should be shown. Many films and filmstrips can be rented at very low rates, and in many cases, they can be used rent-free. The use of the overhead projector is particularly valuable in showing the child the location of various buildings in the city and for other similar objectives.

3. Encourage pupils to bring items to school for the purpose of sharing experiences with their classmates. Take an active interest in each project of the pupil, irrespective of how trivial it may seem. Many children are shy because they have been raised in a cultural environment in which at least one parent is a dominant figure.

4. Read many stories and poems to the children. Ask them to react and/or retell the stories. In some cases dramatization of the stories or parts of the stories may be in order.

5. Having resource persons come to the classroom to make simple explanations of various kinds may be appropriate. A fireman, for example, may explain the simple functions of the various equipment and describe his job in general.

Provisions for Aiding Those with Social and/or Emotional Handicaps

1. The key to success in this area is an understanding teacher who by action and example displays a love for all pupils. For many children, the teacher is the only friend they have.

2. Give the child a considerable amount of time for getting acquainted with the school routine. Do not rush him into a large number of group activities or place him in situations which will make him unduly fearful. Assign minor, individual tasks and then issue honest praise for those aspects of the assignment which are completed satisfactorily. Nothing breeds success like success.

3. On some occasions, it is absolutely imperative to remove a child temporarily from a group when he becomes rebellious or uncontrollable. Quiet individual activities should be provided until he is able to rejoin the group and understand his responsibilities toward the total group.

4. Conferences with the parents may be necessary in order to gain deeper insight into the child's home life. Tactful recommendations should be given to the parents regarding any change which should be instituted in the areas of discipline or home duties.

5. If the situation is complex, the school psychologist should be consulted. Seeking professional help for the child through the appropriate channels may also be necessary.

THE APPRAISAL OF READINESS TO READ

There are a number of aspects to keep in mind in determining if a child is ready to begin formal reading instruction. The results of reading readiness tests, informal observations, and the findings of different intelligence scales are the important ingredients used in finding this information. In the section which follows, there is a discussion of the place and value of each of these factors.

Reading Readiness Tests

Reading readiness tests are designed primarily to provide a suggestion with respect to the nature of specific weaknesses and as an aid in the development of particular plans for enhancing various facets of readiness for reading. One should remember, however, that most reading readiness tests appear to evaluate skills and abilities which are highly related to those found in some items found in the lower levels of intelligence tests. The studies of Bremer[3] and Karlin[7] reveal that the correlation between reading test scores and achievement test scores are not significant and thus seem to indicate that the predictive value of readiness tests is low. Karlin, for example, discovered the reading readiness test data from an experiment involving 100 selected children was only about 4 per cent superior to teacher prediction made without the presence of the readiness data. The results of the readiness tests, however, are of particular value to the beginning teacher. Since she has had limited observational experience, the scores serve to substantiate or refute her feelings about the child.

In discussing the administration of reading readiness tests with many teachers, the impression is given that there is a considerable amount of misunderstanding with regard to *when* the tests should be given. The testing of all children during one particular week during the school year is open to serious debate. Why waste time giving the test to a child when observation clearly indicates that he cannot make a suitable score on the test? Tests should be given only to those children who, in the judgment of the teacher, can perform satisfactorily on the test.

At the present time, there are a number of reading readiness tests on the market which are used by large numbers of teachers.

The *Harrison-Stroud Reading Readiness Test* (Houghton Mifflin Company) has subsections dealing with context and auditory clues, visual discrimination, auditory discrimination, using the context, and using symbols.

One of the most popular tests is the *Lee-Clark Reading Readiness Test* (California Test Bureau). This is a group test printed in one form and contains four subtests which measure the ability to match letters, to follow directions, to note similarities among selected words, and to understand the meaning of words.

The *Metropolitan Readiness Tests* (Harcourt, Brace & World, Inc.) are available in two forms and consist of subtests which measure the child's ability to understand words, comprehension of words and sentences, informational background, level of visual perception, number discrimination ability, and visual and motor ability.

The revised edition of the *American School Reading Readiness Test* (Bobbs-Merrill Company, Inc.) is a test of visual discrimination involving letters and letter combinations; a test of the subject's ability to recognize simple objects; an instrument to measure the ability to reconstruct geometric forms from memory; and an aid in discovering the child's ability to follow directions.

The *Gates MacGinitie Readiness Skills Test* (Teachers College Press) can be used at the end of kindergarten or at the beginning of the first grade. The following areas are assessed: listening comprehension; auditory discrimination; visual discrimination; following directions; letter recognition; visual-motor coordination; auditory blending; and word recognition.

A number of publishers of basal materials supply reading readiness tests. These tests have value for the teacher and should be administered according to the conditions which have been described previously.

In recent years several other instruments have been developed which are being used by some teachers for assessing a child's capability in overall readiness for reading and language development. The *Frostig Test of Visual Perception* (Follett), the *Beery-Buktenica Developmental Test of Visual-Motor Integration* (Follett), and the *McGahan Early Detection Inventory* (Follett) are being used by some school systems. The latter test is designed to screen a child's readiness in the areas of social, emotional, motor, and intellectual development. The *Screening Tests for Identifying Children with Specific Language Disability* (Educators Publishing Service) is designed for use with pupils from grades one to four.

Informal Means of Observation

The appraisal of the present status of each child through day-to-day observations should not be minimized. The information gained can be of help in deciding which children can work together profitably and can serve as a guide in the identification of those children who are ready for beginning reading activities.

In order for observational procedures to be of value, it is imperative to know the characteristics of potentially successful readers. Since it is agreed that there are a number of important elements to keep in mind, the development of a simple yet comprehensive checklist should be undertaken for use with each child. The following list of questions may well serve as a guide.

PHYSICAL QUALIFICATIONS

Body Coordination

1. How well are his bodily movements coordinated?
2. Is he able to cut out pictures and follow lines accurately with a pencil or crayon?
3. Is he adept at handling both large and small books?

Visual Development

1. Does he show any signs of eye fatigue which are evidenced by squinting or blinking?
2. What is the condition of his eyes according to the screening examination?
3. Does he appear to hold the book at unrealistic distances when reading?
4. Does he recognize the likenesses and differences among figures, words, and objects?

Auditory Development

1. Does he hear the likenesses and differences among different kinds of words and phrases?
2. Does his attention span indicate that listening may be difficult?

Oral Speech Patterns

1. Are immature speech patterns such as the use of "baby talk" in evidence?
2. Is it difficult for him to pronounce simple sounds?
3. Does he evidence any problems such as stuttering?

SOCIAL AND EMOTIONAL ADJUSTMENT

1. Is he relaxed in the class situation?
2. Does he appear not to want to "mix" with his peers?
3. Does he seem to be happy and alert?
4. Is he polite and courteous when others are talking?
5. Is he prone to follow directions immediately?
6. Do his classmates respect his contributions?
7. Does he stay with a task until it is finished?
8. Are there any indications of either overaggressive or shy attitudes?
9. Does he accept changes in the school routine without being upset?
10. Is he willing to share materials without being told?

MENTAL DEVELOPMENT

1. Does he appear to have a good memory?
2. Is it possible for him to relate the events of a simple story in order?
3. Can he solve simple problems which appear in day-to-day school life?

4. Do his creative abilities, such as drawing to illustrate an idea or concept, seem to be at a level with the "average" child of his age?

INTERESTS AND ATTITUDES BACKGROUND

1. Is the child interested in books and reading in general?
2. Does he appear interested in the new books which are placed on the library table?
3. Does he know numerous stories and poems?
4. Is there evidence that the child has been to a large number of places and has participated in a number of activities with his family?
5. Is he interested in bringing books from home and sharing them with his classmates?
6. Does he make a noticeable response to any new pictures which have been placed on the bulletin board?
7. Does he appear to like to have stories read to him?

LANGUAGE DEVELOPMENT

1. Is he able to pronounce simple words clearly and properly?
2. Does he use a large variety of words in general conversation with both the teacher and other classmates?
3. Does he speak in full sentence patterns rather than in short, choppy sentences?
4. Are the words found in the pre-primer and readiness materials a part of his listening and speaking vocabulary?
5. Is he able to retell a story in his own words?

If positive responses can be made for a vast majority of the items, the child is a good reading prospect; however, if there are several negative items, it will be necessary to incorporate several of the suggestions given in an earlier part of this chapter into the teaching program for individual children who have specific needs. While not all of the foregoing items may be applicable to any given child, one should be careful to notice every child in terms of his total behavior. The teacher who keeps careful records with regard to each child is much more apt to make an accurate judgment of his true readiness status than the teacher who is content to go on general impressions. The best prediction of a pupil's future success in reading is based on composite pieces of information from readiness tests, intelligence tests, and the teacher's own careful, informal, and regular observation of his abilities.

The Use of Intelligence Scales

An assessment of each child's mental age and intelligence quotient is an important consideration in attempting to judge his readiness to read. Numerous investigators have demonstrated that there is a high degree of relationship between mental age and ease in learning to read. While it is possible to learn to read with a mental age of less than six years, the process is difficult and discouraging for many pupils.

Individual intelligence tests such as the *Binet* or the *Wechsler Intelligence Scale for Children* are preferred by many persons; however, due to the time and personnel resources involved in giving the tests, the use of group tests is one means of deriving certain kinds of information relative to mental factors. The following is a list of group tests which have been used in some schools:

Pintner-Cunningham Primary Mental Test (Harcourt, Brace & World, Inc.)
SRA Primary Mental Abilities (Science Research Associates)
Detroit Beginning First Grade Intelligence Test (Harcourt, Brace & World, Inc.)
California Test of Mental Maturity (California Test Bureau)
Kuhlmann-Anderson Intelligence Test (Education Test Bureau)

A careful study of the results of the various tests should be made in accordance with the instructions given by persons responsible for constructing the tests.

Summary

The term, "reading readiness," indicates that a given child has reached a stage in his educational development when he is able to read without any noticeable physical or emotional discomfort. The evaluation of readiness should be conducted through the use of reading readiness tests, informal teacher-made checklists, the astute observation of the teacher, and the use of individual and group intelligence scales. Those children who have obvious limitations should be provided with activities and experiences which will serve to strengthen their level of readiness and thus hasten the time when formal reading experiences can begin.

Selected References

1. Barbe, Walter. *Educator's Guide to Personalized Reading Instruction.* Englewood Cliffs, New Jersey: Prentice-Hall, Inc., 1961, Chap. 7.
2. Bond, Guy L. and Eva Bond Wagner. *Teaching the Child to Read.* New York: The Macmillan Company, 1966, Chap. 2.
3. Bremer, Neville, "Do Readiness Tests Predict Success in Reading?" *Elementary School Journal,* LIX (January, 1959), 222–24.
4. DeBoer, John J. and Martha Dallman. *The Teaching of Reading.* New York: Holt, Rinehart and Winston, Inc., 1964, Chaps. 5A and 5B.
5. Dechant, Emerald V. *Improving the Teaching of Reading.* Englewood Cliffs, New Jersey: Prentice-Hall, Inc., 1964, Chap. 7.

6. Gates, Arthur I., "The Necessary Mental Age for Beginning Reading," *Elementary School Journal,* XXXVII (March, 1937), 497–508.

7. Karlin, Robert, "The Prediction of Reading Success and Reading-Readiness Tests," *Elementary English,* XXIV (May, 1957), 320–22.

8. McKim, Margaret G., and Helen Caskey. *Guiding Growth in Reading.* New York: The Macmillan Company, 1963, Chap. 3.

9. Morphett, Mabel V. and Carleton Wasburne, "When Should Children Begin to Read?" *Elementary School Journal,* XXI (March, 1931), 496–503.

10. Nila, Sister Mary, O.S.F., "Foundations of a Successful Reading Program," *Education,* LXXIII (May, 1953), 543–55.

11. Russell, David H. *Children Learn to Read.* Waltham, Massachusetts: Blaisdell Publishing Company, 1961, Chap. 6.

12. Smith, Henry P. and Emerald V. Dechant. *Psychology in Teaching Reading.* Englewood Cliffs, New Jersey: Prentice-Hall, Inc., 1961, Chap. 4.

13. Smith, Nila Benton. *Reading Instruction for Today's Children.* Englewood Cliffs, New Jersey: Prentice-Hall, Inc., 1963, Chap. 16.

14. Witty, Paul A., Alma Moore Freeland and Edith H. Crotberg. *The Teaching of Reading.* Boston: D. C. Heath and Company, 1966, Chap. 5.

3

Establishing Effective Primary Reading Instruction

As indicated in the previous chapter, the sequential teaching of reading skills may begin at that point where the child shows a definite desire to want to read. Among other things, he should have developed a wide vocabulary and be able to demonstrate the ability to speak in complete sentences and to follow simple directions. A thorough assessment of the pupil's ability to discriminate likenesses and differences in sounds and objects should be made through the use of standardized and teacher-made devices. The results of these instruments and the checklist described earlier will lend insight into many areas where the child needs further help. Unless he has demonstrated a real interest in learning tc read and has a sufficient level of readiness for the reading act, the formal teaching of reading skills may be a tragic mistake and may cause the young child to be fearful of reading at a later date.

This chapter is designed to help the teacher formulate objectives for the primary reading program and to explain the role of the following areas in the total program of primary reading instruction: oral reading, silent reading, grouping practices, functional reading, recreatory reading, and materials for use in a primary reading program. The steps involved in a developmental reading lesson are discussed near the close of the chapter. A brief summary of the total subject concludes the section.

OBJECTIVES OF THE TEACHER IN THE PRIMARY
READING PROGRAM

Educators have long since determined that learning to read is not a simple task, but rather one which is complex in nature. The approach to instruction, therefore, is one which involves a large number of techniques and approaches and should result in the establishment of a number of objectives to meet the needs of the various children enrolled in the primary grades. Several significant objectives are suggested and explained in the section which follows.

Analyze and Strengthen the Child's Attitudes
Toward Reading and Himself

Very early in the instructional program, efforts should be initiated to discover what the pupil's present viewpoints are with respect to the total act of reading. This information can be obtained through the use of interest inventories and careful observation. If undesirable attitudes are noted, the construction of a series of experiences which will serve to build acceptable feelings and lead him to be curious about books and what they contain is necessary. A few children at *every* socio-economic level are found to have limited interest in wanting to learn to read. For these children, a real challenge confronts the teacher, since unless the pupils develop a sincere desire to want to read, the further work of the teacher will be disappointing and frustrating.

The dedicated teacher who enjoys reading herself and who in turn reads to her pupils will help to instill a love for reading and inspire her students to grasp the excitement which surrounds the reading act.

For the pupils who have had a limited background in reading, provision should be made for a good reading atmosphere: a book corner with a large number of interesting and stimulating picture volumes; bulletin boards which will arouse a pupil's interest through the use of posters; announcements and pictures; and the use of records, puppets, and audio-visual aids to further stimulate the child's interest in reading.

Develop the Verbal Facility of Each Child to the Maximum Level

Investigations relating to the speech and reading growth patterns of children indicate that a given boy or girl cannot cope adequately with a given word unless that word is a part of his or her speaking vocabulary. Typically, the young child may have a speaking acquaintance with 2,500 words or more before he is able to read simple words. Teachers and parents should encourage pupils to speak in many situations such as asking them to describe objects, explain events, and discuss problems. A good language pattern on the part of all adults who deal with children is an absolute prerequisite for the building of an effective language facility. The use of charts and various commercial language experience tools can aid in the enlargement of verbal facility.

Help the Pupil to Develop Adequate Listening Skills

For a child to attain satisfactory growth in reading, it is necessary for him to be able to hear likenesses and differences in sounds. The enlargement of his speaking vocabulary is achieved through listening to the many different words which he hears from his peers and adults. Training should be given to the child through the use of records, rhymes, jingles, poems, and songs. Attention should be directed to the differences between two words which he confuses. "Word family" games such as one in which one pupil says a word and the next pupil has to say a word which begins the same way challenges the child to listening; therefore, formal listening activities must be conducted only when a true audience situation exists.

In order to build a sound, sequential program of listening skills, certain principles should be remembered:

1. Build an interest in the topic which is to be presented and establish an environment of readiness in order that the pupils will *want* to listen.

2. A purpose for listening must be constructed. If the objective is to follow the directions to the nearest fire exit, be sure to transfer this intent to the minds of the pupils.

3. The length of time for a period of sustained listening must be kept relatively brief and in keeping with the attention span of the vast majority of the pupils.

4. The physical aspects of the classroom must be analyzed in building listening skills. The placement of children in comfortable chairs in a well-lighted room with a proper temperature is an important consideration.

Expand the Sight Word Vocabulary of Each Pupil

Many reading authorities are of the belief that children should learn a basic stock of 50 to 100 sight words before any type of word attack skill is introduced. These words should be introduced systematically. There are several reasons for the establishment of a sight word vocabulary: a comparison can be made between the visual and auditory similarities of the known words and the new words which he encounters at a later date; a learning set can be established for an analysis of the whole word rather than isolated parts of the word; and a sizable number of words can be learned in a short period of time by this procedure.

Teach the Pupils to Use Several Methods of Word Attack

As explained in Chapter 5, the primary child must be taught to use all of the common word attack skills efficiently: configuration clues, phonetic analysis, structural analysis, context clues, and picture clues. The teacher's responsibility is to show each child the importance of each of these skills and when to use them independently or in combination with other techniques. No one skill (such as phonetic analysis) should be emphasized to the exclusion of all other methods. A balanced word attack program will help to insure that each child will be successful in his attempts to pronounce a large number of unknown words.

Provide a Program of Balanced Practice in Oral and Silent Reading

There are many instances when oral reading is justified and desirable. When adequate preparation is made, oral reading can help particular pupils to build self-confidence and thus result in an enlargement of his personal and social growth. An analysis of a pupil's reading limitations can also be achieved through oral reading. The amount of time spent on oral and silent reading should be based on the content and style of a given selection. A later section of this chapter contains a further discussion of this topic.

Provide Experiences Which Will Help to Develop and Extend Concepts

The development of concepts cannot be left to incidental planning. As an example, the use of a picture of a banana tree is one of the effective means of explaining how bananas actually grow. Comparisons of the characteristics of different animals can be demonstrated through the use of several pictures (i.e., a shaggy lion, a tall giraffe, a small monkey, a long snake). Other audio-visual aids such as filmstrips and films may also be employed for these purposes.

Design and Implement Provisions for Meeting Individual Needs of Pupils

A study of any group of primary children will immediately reveal the fact that wide differences in the realms of intelligence, physical factors, and psychological structure are in evidence. Educational provisions such as various grouping procedures are an absolute "must" if one is to meet these differences. A large number of interesting books on various reading levels should be available.

In order to implement the preceding objectives, one must have a thorough understanding of all of the major facets of the primary reading program. Several of these factors are discussed in the section which follows.

THE PLACE OF ORAL READING IN THE
PRIMARY READING PROGRAM

Early in the 1900's, oral reading was widely equated and, indeed, interpreted as constituting the reading program. During this period, a county or city superintendent of schools evaluated a teacher's capability as a reading instructor in light of the oral reading skills demonstrated by her pupils. "Round-robin" reading was vogue, and all pupils were expected to read aloud during the reading period.

Today, we know that oral reading has a very definite place in the instructional program if proper conditions are present. Much preparation on the part of both the pupil and teacher is necessary if maximum values are to be derived from oral experiences.

Silent reading must precede oral reading unless the objective is primarily that of diagnosis. A child cannot derive pleasure from a reading lesson unless the reading materials are at or below his instructional reading level.

There is little justification for a situation in which the teacher asks every pupil in a class to read orally a common set of materials regardless of the instructional reading levels of the individual pupils. Those who have trouble reading the material are embarrassed, and the better readers are bored by having to listen and wait their turn.

In light of these and other conditions, one should observe a number of considerations when making use of oral readings.

1. An audience situation must prevail. The pupil who is reading should have the feeling that he has information which he wishes to share with others because it is humorous, factual, and/or rhythmical in nature. The remainder of the pupils must be taught to be good listeners (as explained earlier) and to respect the rights of others. The purposes for both the reading and listening experiences must be conveyed to the pupils.

2. Every pupil who is asked to read orally must be prepared for the assignment. The material should contain a minimum of difficult words and the pupil must be able to interpret the meaning and purpose of the writer to his listeners. In order to do this effectively, a thorough orientation with respect to the meaning of various punctuation marks should precede oral reading assignments. Children must understand that they have a responsibility to their listeners and that reading in a monotonous, halting manner is not pleasurable to the rest of the class. Oral reading *must* have meaning.

3. The teacher can provide a good model for her pupils by reading short selections which are on the interest and vocabulary levels of the pupils. Primary children tend to imitate the teacher in many ways, especially with respect to the degree of enthusiasm and meaning which she exhibits when reading orally.

4. The frequent use of a tape recorder is desirable for a number of

reasons. Children like to hear their voices as well as those of their class-mates. Even young children are able to detect their oral reading errors and have a much greater inclination to want to improve their oral reading efficiency. While listening to the tape recordings, a checklist should be used to record the types of errors made by the individual pupils. This information will serve as a guide to the further oral reading instructional needs of the children with regard to such aspects as sight vocabulary, general word attack skills, use of punctuation, and use of context.

5. A careful balance must be maintained regarding the amount of silent and oral reading that is completed during a given period. One should never feel compelled to have every child read orally during the developmental reading period. An alert teacher is much more concerned with fulfilling a total set of objectives instead of attempting to follow a meaningless "barbershop" technique which contributes little to reading growth.

SILENT READING INSTRUCTION

Silent and oral reading take many skills which are common to both areas; however, competency in one area does not necessarily indicate success in the other area. Instruction in silent reading cannot be separated from oral reading. Efficient oral reading takes place a moment after the pupil has recognized any one of a group of words.

Typically, the primary child prefers oral reading over silent reading, since he feels a sense of importance when he hears his own voice. Many pupils feel insecure in silent reading situations because the teacher is not always aware of the exact difficulty which a given child may be experiencing at a given moment.

One of the principal responsibilities of the instructor is that of providing opportunities for each pupil to gain security in silent reading. A number of procedures are described in the section below.

Word Activity Involving Directions

After a child or a group of children have learned a number of words such as "write," "draw," "take," "name," and "point," these words should be placed on strips of tagboard or posterboard in context with other words to form a meaningful phrase which commands the reader to perform a certain duty. Some of the flash strips, for example, may read, "point to the flag," "take your cap to the back of the room," "draw a picture of a snowman," or "name one of the colors." Individual children should be asked to perform the task which is designated on various strips. This type of lesson gives a purpose to a child and demands that silent reading be performed efficiently.

Another lesson involving the following of directions consists of having the children read a brief story in which each sentence of the story is numbered and each sentence is on a different line. A child is obligated to read each line in order to answer such specific questions as, "which sentence tells us the color of Mary's shoes?" or "which line tells us about the size of her shoes?"

Reading for a Purpose

Primary children enjoy silent reading activities if a definite purpose is given for the reading. As an example, the teacher might duplicate a simple story such as the following:

> Bob, Jimmy, Jean, Billy, and Ann were invited to Jill's birthday party. Jill was seven years old. Jill's mother gave some ice cream and cake to each of the children. Everyone had a good time at the party.

Before the story is read by the pupils, one could write a number of questions on the greenboard or on posterboard, such as the following: "What were the names of the five children who were invited to the party?" "What kinds of food did Jill's mother give to the children?" "How old was Jill on her birthday?" These and other questions could be devised from a story of this nature.

After the pupils have had a chance to read the above story silently, individual children could be asked to underline the sentence or sentences which answer a given question.

Short Story Exercise Reading

To give practice in silent reading facility, five or six sentence stories might be duplicated. All words in the stories should be within the experience background of the pupils and each word should be a part of his sight vocabulary. A multiple-choice type question should follow each story, in which the child is expected to place a check beside the appropriate response. An example of one of the stories and the accompanying question might read as follows:

> Miss Brown said, "Boys and girls, it is time for recess. What game should we play today?" The children liked recess time very much. "I would like to play 'keep away' with our large red ball," said Betty.
> "I think we should play a game with our softball," said Mary.

"We cannot play both games during recess," said Miss Brown. "Let's play with the red ball today and the softball tomorrow."

Betty wanted to play with the softball
                           the large red ball

Remember that the proper selection of interesting story material on the instructional reading levels of the pupils is one of the most significant factors to keep in mind in motivating children to improve silent reading skills. Careful observation of each child must be maintained during all silent reading activities in order that a constant evaluation of his reading strengths and limitations may be classified and dealt with accordingly.

THE GROUPING OF PUPILS

One of the most complex problems of educators at all grade levels is the proper grouping of pupils in order to insure maximum educational benefits. Following the revision of the Binet Scale by Terman in 1916, there was a special concern on the part of administrators and teachers with respect to the wide range of mental abilities which existed in individual classrooms. Achievement tests which were devised at a later period indicated that the same wide differences existed in the academic realms. During the past forty years, as many as thirty different classroom grouping organizations have been developed to meet the needs of pupils in reading and other subject areas.

Regardless of the type of grouping procedure employed, it is important to determine the reading status of each pupil in a careful manner. In doing this, examine any records compiled by kindergarten teachers, analyze any statements made by the kindergarten teacher or the pupil's parents, observe the child's overall attitude regarding the reading act, and take note of all the factors which were described on the checklist noted in the previous chapter.

In today's affluent society, it is not uncommon to find many children who have attended kindergarten in a school other than the one in which their first grade experiences are obtained. Some have not been in a kindergarten curriculum while others have had stimulating nursery school instruction and/or participation in a Montessori School. In studying the capabilities of all of the various pupils, the following groups generally emerge:

1. A small group of children who have had actual formal reading instruction at some earlier level and are fairly conversant with many of the sight words normally introduced at the first grade level.

2. Children who have impoverished backgrounds with regard to experiences which are necessary for adequate reading readiness.

3. Children who appear to have a satisfactory level of reading readiness and who can recognize a few words.

4. A very small group of pupils who have been raised in homes where the language is other than English.

There are a number of grouping procedures which are practiced in various parts of the United States; however, the more common ones are those of grouping within the classroom and the ungraded primary. In a few situations, pupils are grouped according to the interests of children with the memberships of the groups kept reasonably flexible. The level of reading ability is a prime consideration in all of the group plans.

Regardless of the grouping plan used for reading instruction, a number of important factors should be kept in mind:

1. Since children grow at vastly different rates, one must be conversant with the teaching techniques which may be used at a number of grade levels.

2. Maximum reading growth can only be achieved when instruction is based on the exact needs of individual pupils. Evaluation must be both periodic and continuous with lesson plans centered especially on the areas which show limitations. No materials have ever been compiled which are so thorough and sequential that they will provide for all of the needs of the pupils.

3. The membership of the groups must be kept flexible. In far too many cases, children who are placed in the low reading group are never moved to the next higher group regardless of growth achieved. Children's learning rates must be paced at all times.

4. Each child must be made to understand his strengths and limitations. Discuss with each child the nature of his errors and why certain practices will serve to improve his skills in the various reading growth areas.

5. The physical arrangement of the room must be studied as a part of the grouping procedures. The chairs must be of the size and type for the pupils who are using them. Hard-of-hearing pupils should be seated near the teacher. The reading groups should be formed in an area which is close to the book supplies and other materials which will be used sometime during the lessons.

6. On some occasions, the necessity may arise for forming small groups of children on the basis of needs or interest. For instance, two or three children from each of the regular reading groups may appear to have difficulty with certain consonant blends. A special helps group should be established and maintained on an "ad hoc" basis until a sufficient level of proficiency has been realized by all of the members of the group.

7. A large number of interesting reading materials must be made available for all of the reading groups. In order to meet the needs of the various pupils, the teacher must be acquainted with a large number of teaching aids in addition to the conventional basal materials. One of the most urgent instructional problems of this age is the placement of the proper materials in the hands of individual pupils at the teachable time.

8. For the highly gifted pupils, individualized instruction may be an excellent technique for adequate pacing of learning. The individualized approach requires that the teacher be thoroughly familiar with a large number of reading materials, and that she organize the reading experiences for each child in order that a sequential development of reading skills is possible.

9. The grouping of all children requires a careful analysis of the reading levels of each pupil. A description of the various levels is as follows:
   Independent level—the highest reading level at which a child reads without help from the teacher. He must demonstrate a comprehension score of at least 90 per cent on both factual and inferential type questions. He should be able to pronounce at least 99 per cent of all running words in a story. There is an absence of tension symptoms such as fingerpainting, lip movements, and frowning.
   Instructional level—the highest reading level at which a child can read with a normal amount of teacher aid. He is able to pronounce correctly 95 to 98 per cent of all running words and is able to demonstrate a comprehension score of from 75 to 89 per cent on both factual and inferential type questions. Oral reading is characterized by normal rhythm and a freedom of tensions.
   Frustration level—a reading level which is characterized by comprehension levels of less than 74 per cent. Many tensions are noticed and there are many omissions, substitutions, and hesitations in oral reading.
   Capacity level—an understanding level which is characterized by an ability to comprehend 75 per cent of material which is read orally by the teacher.

In order to place pupils in the proper groups, the determination of their instructional and frustration levels is absolutely necessary. The use of both standardized tests and informal reading inventories (which are described in Chapter 9) can be employed to derive this information. Standardized reading tests supply scores that are of value in making comparisons of present performance with the local, regional, and national norms which have been established for a given test. The informal reading inventory is an individual measure which yields information relative to a subject's oral and silent reading abilities on a series of selected stories from a graded series of basal readers.

FUNCTIONAL OR WORK-TYPE READING

One of the main products of any worthwhile primary reading program is the construction of functional or work-type reading skills which will result in maximum comprehension levels.

In the primary grades, children should begin to learn how to comprehend and evaluate various reading materials which are on their level. They should learn how to handle books and how to locate materials in them. Very young children can be instructed in the use of the table of contents in order to find the page number of a particular story. Demonstrations should be conducted in the use of the index or glossary which are found in many content area books. After teaching these skills, structured lessons such as the following which demand the use of these skills should be undertaken:

1. There is a very interesting story in your reader entitled, "The Man in the Little Green House." Will you please look in the table of contents and tell me on what page the story begins?

2. Open to the very last page of the book. How many pages are there in your reader?

3. Look at the glossary. On what page of the book would you expect to find some information about George Washington?

4. Which of these words would come first in the glossary: *man, apple, white,* or *body?* (provided, of course, that the words are listed alphabetically)

In content area books such as those in the areas of social studies and science, the pupil is faced with a large amount of factual information. One can help him derive the most information from the materials by asking him to read in order to answer very specific questions which are posed *before* he attempts to read silently.

The following procedures may be followed with individual or small groups of pupils in order that they may derive the most useable information from a given body of materials:

1. Have pupils look at the name of the chapter and the titles of the sub-topics in order that they might become oriented with respect to the nature and kinds of information which are presented.

2. Ask them to write questions which the various sub-topics may suggest. By using this procedure, they will have a *purpose* for reading.

3. Direct them to read the various sections in order to answer the questions which they have compiled. Some pupils should consider only one section at a time, while more advanced primary pupils can consider as many as four or five different sections in one sitting.

Another skill area which is important for efficient reading at the upper primary level is that of selecting the proper book as a source for desired information. The teacher has the responsibility for demonstrating the different types of books which are available to the children for social studies or a science unit. Through inductive teaching, pupils should reason, for example, that a book entitled, *How to Grow Flowers,* would be a more apt reference for finding information with respect to different kinds of flower bulbs than would a book entitled, *Sights and Scenes from Norway.*

RECREATORY READING

As older primary children gain facility in the various reading skills, it is only natural that they will want to read in various trade books for pleasure during the free reading period. In order to provide this opportunity, titles of books should be suggested to the school librarian or principal which may be of interest to the pupils in given classrooms. Recommended book lists may be secured from university professors who instruct courses in children's literature or from the librarian of the children's book section of the local public or university library. Additional information may be secured from the officials who are in charge of the State Reading Circle activities.

Pupils should be encouraged to visit the local public library and secure a library card and ask for information relating to the policies of the library with respect to borrowing procedures. Some rural areas have access to bookmobiles. In some cases, a teacher may wish to check out as many as thirty to fifty books at a time from a local library for the use of the pupils. If a large volume of books is collected at one time, care should be taken to see that the books are on many different reading levels and are on a large number of subjects.

The participation of pupils in the State Reading Circle or other similar reading clubs is highly desirable. Children are led to read books in many different areas and to develop a more intense love of books and for reading in general. However, no pupil should be forced or required to be a member of such groups.

Children will have a greater desire to engage in recreatory reading if books are read to them. In some cases, it may be more desirable to read an entire story or selection, while at other times the reading of the beginning of a story to build curiosity may be in order. Reading to children immediately following a short recess or activity period serves to "settle" them and put them in a mood for the developmental lesson which may follow.

MATERIALS FOR USE IN PRIMARY READING PROGRAMS

Materials are generally divided into two groups: those which are published by commercial concerns (such as readers, practice books, and charts), and those which are constructed by the teacher. Since learning to read is complex, the methods and materials used in any given program must be varied and of the nature which will meet the widely varying needs of individual pupils. (A description of many related aids currently available can be found in the appendix.) No one set of either the commercial or teacher-made varieties is so complete that other materials are not needed.

The core of materials used in most primary grades consists of basal materials which have been compiled by reading authorities. Typically, a number of readers beginning with the pre-primer level are provided and are constructed from a developmental, sequential point of view. Precise lesson suggestions are provided in the teacher's manual for each reader and workbook series. Vocabulary is controlled and various words are systematically repeated in later books to provide needed practice.

While there are a number of obvious advantages for using basal materials, care must be taken with regard to the use made of the aids. Manuals cannot and should not be used as "the last word." The teaching outlines must be regarded as suggested lessons and suitable variations must be undertaken to meet the needs of pupils. *Remember:* the instructor is teaching children, not the book.

The basal material most frequently misused is the workbook or practice book. Properly used, these materials serve the important function of providing additional practice for the pupil who is deficient in some significant reading skill. In a few cases, the practice of asking all children to complete a given page in a workbook may be justified; however, in the vast majority of the cases, adequate reasoning cannot be found. The policy of demanding that all pupils in a given room complete all pages ultimately results in boredom for the more alert pupils and discouragement for the disabled readers.

Teacher-made materials such as experience charts and bulletin board posters serve an important adjunct to the basal program. Children are able to identify with the stories which are found on experience charts because they have had the opportunity to dictate the sentences. These charts can be used very profitably in grades one, two, and three. Attention to new study units can be heightened through the use of special bulletin boards which contain pictures and related words which pertain to the unit. Lesson charts which provide examples of a word attack skill generalization can be produced and used with a small group of pupils who need that particular practice.

THE DIRECTED READING LESSON

The *first* step in a well planned reading lesson is the development of readiness for the story or poem to be read. Attention should be drawn to the title of the story, and the experiential backgrounds of the pupils should be explored regarding the concepts mentioned in the title. For example, in the story, "The Circus Parade," the children might be asked such questions as: "How many of you have seen a parade?" "Who did you see marching in the parade?" "On what street did you see the parade?" A careful development of readiness for the story helps the child develop an interest and a purpose for reading.

The *second* step in the lesson is that of the introduction of new words and phrases which occur in the story as well as a review of old vocabulary. In the case of words which have been learned previously, various sentences might be constructed which call for the use of these words at various places in the sentences. The following procedure is a means which one might use to review old words:

1. Print the review words on the greenboard. (Example: *snow, o'clock, ball, lunch, morning.*)

2. Print the following sentences on the board:
   The _____ was white and cold.
   I threw the _____ to John and we played a game.
   At noon we eat our _____.
   This _____ I came to school.
   School begins at nine _____.
   Have the pupils read each sentence silently. Ask individual children to come to the board and point to the word which goes on a particular blank.

List the new words to be found in the story on the greenboard or on a piece of posterboard. Use each of the words in a sentence, making sure that all of the words in the sentence (other than the new word) are within the sight vocabulary of the children. Emphasize the use of the appropriate word analysis techniques for attacking the new words (as explained in Chapter 5 of this book). Ask them to think of the meaning of the new words as they are used in the sentences. When the pupils can pronounce the new word and can use it in context, ask them to use each new word in a sentence of their own either orally or written.

The *third* step consists of guided reading. As a "starter" for the guided reading, one may point to a picture and ask a question such as "Can you tell from the picture where Mr. Brown is going? Let's read the story silently to find out." If the selection is quite brief and the pupils have an adequate attention span, one may wish to have them read the story without any type of interruption. At the conclusion of the reading, a discussion should be held to answer the question which was posed at the outset of the story. If the story is quite long and somewhat complex, the different sections may be read orally or silently or by both methods. If there are parts of the story which are especially humorous or exciting, oral reading may be more appropriate than silent reading. On the other hand, silent reading should be used when the selection is informational in nature. The general make-up of the story should dictate the methods which can be appropriately used.

The *fourth* step is perhaps the most important segment of the entire lesson. At this stage, skill development in such areas as meaning vocabulary, word analysis, and different comprehension segments are stressed through the use of appropriate exercises in the practice book or by means of worksheets which have been previously prepared. In assigning exercises of this nature, several important considerations should be remembered:

1. Explain precisely to the pupils what they are to do and how to do it. Mistakes are compounded when there is a lack of direction and supervision on the part of the teacher.

2. As indicated earlier, exercises should be for a distinct purpose such as needed practice on a skill which has been previously introduced. The lesson may also be justified if a new skill is being introduced. One should never assign "seatwork" just to keep pupils busy.

3. See that the exercises are corrected in order that the pupil may understand his areas of strengths and his limitations. In some cases the teacher may wish to correct the practice sheet alone—in other instances the teacher and the child together should check the work. Depending on the complexity and the length of the lesson, one may be justified occasionally in having the pupil check his own work. The latter practice may result in the child having a more intimate understanding of the types of errors he is committing.

4. A careful record should be kept of each child's progress in the various skill areas. Various special "help" groups may be established on a temporary basis from time to time for those pupils whose records indicate a need for special lessons to overcome specific limitations.

The specific skills relating to word analysis and comprehension instruction in the primary grades are explained fully in Chapters 5 and 6 respectively.

The *fifth* and final step in the developmental lesson is that of enrichment activities. In some cases these activities might consist of drawing a picture of some character in the story, dramatizing a scene from the story, or making a diorama depicting some action which took place in the story. Provide the pupils with names of other books which have stories which are related to the one discussed during the lesson. Many of these suggested books and stories are listed in the manuals for basal reading materials.

Summary

In order to help insure the development of successful readers at the upper grade and high school levels, the primary teacher must develop objectives for her reading program which provide for sequential instruction in the basic reading skills of vocabulary, word attack, and comprehension.

The needs of individual pupils must be recognized and met through careful grouping procedures.

Oral reading and silent reading activities are important aspects of any well developed program; however, certain principles must be considered when making use of these techniques. A careful analysis of the story to be studied will dictate the amount of emphasis which should be given to these procedures.

The use of the glossary and the table of contents are important functional reading skills and should be included in later primary reading instruction. Recreatory reading should be emphasized at all grade levels by the introduction of many types of trade books to the pupils. These books should represent many different kinds of stories and include selections written at varying levels of difficulty.

Materials for the primary reading program consist of those sold commercially and those made by the teacher. Both types are important and should be included in all instructional procedures.

The directed reading lesson consists of five steps: First, development of readiness; Second, study of old and new vocabulary; Third, guided reading; Fourth, skill development; and Fifth, enrichment activities.

Selected References

1. Carter, Homer L. J. and McGinnis, Dorothy J. *Teaching Individuals to Read.* Boston: D. C. Heath and Company, 1962. Chap. 4.
2. Dechant, Emerald V. *Improving the Teaching of Reading.* Englewood Cliffs, N.J.: Prentice-Hall, Inc., 1964. Chap. 9.
3. Heilman, Arthur W. *Principles and Practices of Teaching Reading.* Columbus: Charles E. Merrill Books, Inc., 1967. Chaps. 3 and 4.
4. McKee, Paul. *Reading: A Program of Instruction for the Elementary School.* Boston: Houghton Mifflin Company, 1966. Chap. 3.
5. McKim, Margaret G. and Caskey, Helen. *Guiding Growth in Reading.* New York: The Macmillan Company, 1963. Chaps. 6, 7, 8, and 9.
6. Smith, Henry P. and Dechant, Emerald. *Psychology in Teaching Reading.* Englewood Cliffs, N.J.: Prentice-Hall, Inc., 1961. Chap. 14.
7. Smith, Nila B. *Reading Instruction for Today's Children.* Englewood Cliffs, N.J.: Prentice-Hall, Inc., 1963. Chap. 15.
8. Tinker, Miles A. and McCullough, Constance M. *Teaching Elementary Reading.* New York: Appleton-Century-Crofts, Inc., 1962. Chaps. 20 and 21.
9. Witty, Paul A., Freeland, Alma Moore, and Grotberg, Edith H. *The Teaching of Reading.* Boston: D. C. Heath and Company, 1966. Chap. 9.

4

Reading in the Intermediate and Upper Grades

A program of reading instruction at the middle and upper grade levels is characterized by the development of the more complex skills in reading, such as reading to differentiate between fact and opinion; reading maps, graphs, and charts; and reading in order to make a generalization. Functional and recreatory reading grows in importance as wide reading is encountered in the various subject content areas.

Problems in reading instruction are typically encountered due to the fact that the range of reading abilities widens, thus causing individual teachers and administrators to search for appropriate means for meeting the varying needs of the pupils. To care for this situation, a number of grouping procedures have been devised, such as the use of the individualized approach, the Joplin Plan, and the three-group plan (which is commonly employed in self-contained classrooms).

Additional questions relating to the specific reading skills to be taught at the middle and upper grade levels are a source of controversy. Many teachers are also concerned about such matters as the relative importance of oral and silent reading, the rate of reading, and the kinds of materials which should be used in the reading program.

In order to emphasize the most important segments of reading instruction at these grade levels, a discussion of the following topics is included in this chapter: (1) aims of reading instruction for the intermediate and upper grades (2) providing for individual differences in the reading program (3) the roles of oral and silent reading (4) developing an effective reading rate (5) functional and recreatory reading (6) the teacher and the developmental reading program (7) the use of various reading materials, and (8) a summary of the total discussion.

AIMS OF READING INSTRUCTION FOR THE INTERMEDIATE AND UPPER GRADES

Any well-formulated reading instructional program should be characterized by a number of common objectives. All teachers at the intermediate and upper grade levels must be committed to these goals if their pupils are to become efficient readers. A discussion of the most important of these goals follows.

Continue the Program of Continuous Evaluation to Discover the Present Achievement Levels of Pupils

If the teacher should instruct the child on the basis of his present abilities, one must use various standardized and teacher-made tests to determine a given child's competency in the following areas:

1. oral reading skills, including phrasing, pitch, and stress
2. degree of facility in sight word vocabulary
3. word attack skills, especially phonetic and structural analysis
4. level of ability to profit from listening activities
5. use of specialized sources such as the encyclopedia and *World Almanac*
6. rate of silent reading employed for different types of reading material
7. the various comprehension skill strands (as described in Chapter 6)
8. general desire for engaging in recreatory reading experiences.

Provide a Wide Variety of Reading Materials in Both the Content and Trade Book Areas

Since pupils have divergent reading abilities and interests, one must be alert to see that ample stocks of materials are available. Children should have proper guidance in the selection of books in order to secure a well balanced reading "diet." Both hardback and paperback books should be included in the appendix section of this volume. Ask the school or city librarian for suggestions with respect to additional purchases which might be made.

Continue a Program of Sequential Reading Instruction

Intermediate and upper grade teachers must accept the philosophy that organized instruction in building reading skills does not end at grade three or grade six. The editors of the various basal materials series indicate in the teachers' manuals the specific skills which should be introduced and reviewed at the various grade levels. Additional information concerning these skills is found in the different chapters in this book which relate to word analysis, comprehension, and reading in the content areas.

Provide Experiences for Those Children Who Are Intellectually Gifted

Many teachers follow the convenient practice of planning lessons in all of the curriculum areas which appeal to the large segment of pupils who are reading at or near grade level. Attention must be given to gifted pupils through the use of enrichment activities which make use of a large number of stimulating and challenging materials. (Additional information on this topic is included near the close of Chapter 9.)

Aid Children in Increasing Rate of Reading

At about the fourth grade level, pupils are expected to read many different materials in the content area subjects. They should be shown that one reads at different rates for different purposes—slow, deliberate reading for details and skimming when reading for a general idea. Detailed suggestions for helping children with this aspect are included in a later part of this chapter.

Extend Each Child's Facility in the Use of Work-Study Skills

Since intermediate and upper grade pupils are expected to use a number of sources for securing information, appropriate instruction should be given for the following activities:

1. using the index, table of contents, and appendix
2. interpreting charts, graphs, maps, tables, and figures
3. using encyclopedias and similar references efficiently
4. making use of the different aspects of the library including the use of the card catalogue

Encourage and Stimulate Pupils to Engage in Recreational Reading

One of the important products of any reading program is a love of reading for pleasure and recreation. Personal adjustment is intensified when a pupil can identify with a story character with whom he has become acquainted. The use of story hours and book fairs can do much to promote this objective.

PROVIDING FOR INDIVIDUAL DIFFERENCES IN THE READING PROGRAM

In order to provide for the obvious wide range of reading abilities in the heterogeneous classroom, a large number of instructional procedures have been devised over the past century to care for the individual needs of pupils. With the possible exception of the role of phonetic instruction, there is no phase of the reading program which is more controversial than the problem of organizing for instruction. Professional literature is full of accounts of research studies regarding this area, but much of the data appears to be inconclusive.

Child psychologists and sophisticated researchers are very quick to point out that pupils have many varying needs and that they cannot be grouped on the basis of any one particular aspect. There is no such thing as a purely homogeneous group, since any two persons have different abilities and aptitudes. The use of grouping plans, at best, only serves to narrow the range of reading abilities.

Principles of Effective Grouping in the Middle and Upper Grades

If it is agreed that grouping is necessary for effective instruction, what guideposts should be followed in developing these procedures?

First, pupils must be allowed to move from one group to another as circumstances dictate. If evidence is not available that flexibility is practiced, children are not being motivated properly. Far too many teachers place pupils in their respective reading groups in September and, regardless of how little or how much reading growth takes place, they are still in the same group at the close of the school year. This situation should not be tolerated.

Second, the physical features of the room must be taken into consideration in determining the feasibility of grouping practices. Tables and. chairs must be movable so they can be easily arranged to accommodate any grouping formation. Book shelves should be located in close proximity to the activities of the reading groups.

Third, the presence of a large number of interesting books which have been written on a number of reading levels is an absolute "must." Even the most ambitious teacher cannot be effective if she is restricted by a lack of suitable materials.

Fourth, the interests of the pupils must be considered in the grouping procedures. If children are to be active participants in any one group, a careful analysis of their interests must be made through the use of informal interest inventories and through careful observation. Knowing the interests of each child helps in planning meaningful lessons for him.

Other factors such as the enrollment in each class and the teacher's background and experience in the teaching of reading must be considered. In any situation, there should never be more groups than any one teacher can handle at any given time.

Since the results of many studies involving grouping procedures have not provided definitive answers, several of the more common grouping methods are discussed in the following section. After consideration has been given to the principles of effective grouping which have been previously discussed, a given teacher may choose to select one of the following methods after considering carefully the advantages and limitations of each plan.

The Joplin Plan

The "Joplin Plan" is an intergrade method of grouping pupils in grades four, five, and six, in which each of the pupils are sent to reading classes on the basis of reading achievement test scores and the observations of the teachers and administrators. Under this arrangement, for example, a fifth grade child may be sent to any reading level class from three through seven or eight. This plan has been used in Joplin, Missouri, and a number of other cities for several years.

Several advantages can be claimed for this type of grouping. The range of reading achievement levels represented in each of the reading level classes is narrowed considerably by the intergrade ability procedures. Because of this condition, it is possible for the individual teachers to instruct from a common core of materials. (One must remember, however, that the use of the plan does not eliminate the need for some further differentiation of instruction.)

Children are able to succeed in the program, since they are working at their appropriate instructional levels. Due to the fact that many disabled readers have short-term goals, the importance of even a small amount of reading gain is vital.

Some limitations appear to be inherent in the use of this grouping plan. The correlation between the actual reading needs of the pupils in the content areas and the nature of the reading instruction offered by the special reading teacher may not be positive. Communication among teachers is difficult, because of the large numbers of children enrolled in the various classrooms and the number of extracurricular activities of individual teachers. In some instances the possibility of social problems exists when sixth grade pupils are placed in the same reading class with groups of fourth grade pupils. There is a considerable range of latitude in social maturity and intellectual interests among groups of this nature.

A variation of the "Joplin Plan" has been used in a number of schools with much success. Under one such arrangement, three teachers at one middle or upper grade level divide all of the pupils at that grade level into three groups on the basis of ability. One teacher is assigned the low group, one the middle group, and one the upper group. This plan appears to be successful when close communication is maintained among the various teachers. In summary, the "Joplin Plan" is an outstanding means of meeting the individual reading needs of the middle and upper grade child as long as one understands that there is a need for further differentiation of instruction and for correlation of efforts among all teachers involved.

The Individualized Approach

Since this approach is described in full in a later chapter, a short description of the plan will suffice at this point. Each child in a particular class reads from a book which he has chosen which is on his ability level and is of interest to him. Individual interviews are held by the teacher with each child at least once a week and a careful record is kept of his progress in the reading skill areas. The plan may be very successful if the teacher is imaginative, energetic, and has a broad background with respect to the reading skills which must be taught at a particular grade level. There should be an average of fifteen books available for each child enrolled in the program. The materials should be concerned with many different topics and on varying levels of difficulty.

Self-Contained Classroom Grouping

The most common means of meeting the individual needs of pupils in reading appears to be the practice of teachers who group their children within their own classrooms. Soon after the opening of the school year, the teacher generally examines each pupil's school record to get an impression of his reading ability as reflected by reading achievement test scores and the comments of previous teachers. In many cases additional standardized and informal instruments are administered in order to learn each child's *present* reading status. Groups are formed after a careful study has been made of all the information obtained from these sources.

If one uses the self-contained classroom grouping procedures, several very important factors must be remembered:

1. The membership of the reading groups *must* be kept flexible. All pupils must be made to feel that they will be moved to the next higher reading level as their abilities improve. The pupil's attitude toward a change to a new group must be carefully considered. Some pupils are aided by moving them to a lower group where they might succeed, while other pupils are so thoroughly humiliated by the action that they lose interest in trying to improve their reading skills.

2. There is nothing sacred about the number of groups which should be formed. While three groups appear to be the most common number— two groups, four groups, or even one large group may be entirely justifiable.

3. One might form special help groups occasionally which would include participants from all of the regularly established groups. As an example, several pupils may need help in some phonetic analysis skill. The group should be disbanded as soon as the limitation with which that particular teaching was concerned has been eliminated.

4. There is no such thing as a purely homogeneous group; therefore, further differentiation of instruction must be a significant aspect of any efficient reading instructional program.

There is no single best way which provides for the individual differences of all children in the classroom. The "Joplin Plan" may be the best procedure for one community while individualized reading under certain circumstances may be the best method to use in another school or city. Any kind of grouping is efficient if each child within the group becomes an independent reader with satisfactory facility in using the different word attack techniques and in demonstrating his ability with regard to the various comprehension skill strands. Study carefully all of the advantages *and* limitations of any grouping program before adopting it.

THE ROLE OF SILENT AND ORAL READING

Silent and oral reading are important aspects of any given reading program. Nearly all of the skills which are necessary for silent reading are also imperative for effective oral reading. A word or a group of words in print cannot be read orally unless the reader has recognized the word a split-second previously. For both skills it is necessary for the reader to have a good facility in word recognition skills, a suitable meaning vocabulary, and the ability to derive different meanings from the printed page.

Learning to read well orally involves much more than learning to read silently. The oral reader must be a good silent reader to be sure, but he must also be able to convey the message to his audience in a meaningful way. A child might well have sufficient skill in silent reading to comprehend at a certain level, but cannot read the same material orally in such a manner that a given audience can comprehend the meaning satisfactorily. For these reasons, specific training must be provided in *both* the silent and oral reading areas.

The use of oral reading experiences can be of great aid in helping to diagnose the difficulties a pupil experiences in silent reading. During oral reading one can detect difficulties such as insertion of words or phrases; skipping lines and titles; omission of words or letters; and poor phrasing.

Unless oral reading is designed for diagnostic purposes, the reading material should be at or below a given child's reading instructional level. With this point of view, the practice of having all children read a story or a poem orally on the "installment plan" cannot be justified. Oral reading must always be an activity which serves to communicate information to others and not one which is done for pure drill.

A question which appears to bother a large segment of teachers is one which deals with the amount of time which should be spent on oral and silent reading at any particular grade level. There is no easy answer to this question, since a number of factors must be considered. The individual needs of pupils, the materials available, the amount of silent reading done in classes, and the teacher's own background of experience in teaching reading are important factors which should be considered. As much as three-fourths of the reading period at the primary level may be given over profitably to oral reading activities, while at the middle and upper grade levels as little as one-fourth or one-third of the time may be used for oral reading. If as much as three-fourths of the reading period is allocated for oral reading at the sixth grade level, for example, the teacher in question might well re-examine her goals to see if ample justification is present for her practices in light of the suggestions and principles which are outlined and discussed in this section.

Principles of Oral Reading Instruction

If oral reading activities are to be undertaken at the middle and upper grade levels, several important considerations should be remembered:

1. Pupils should always give evidence that they can read a selection silently before they make any attempt to read it orally. Except for diagnostic purposes, no child should be asked to read a selection orally unless he has read it silently.

2. As a daily routine, pupils *should not* be asked to follow in their own books a selection that is being read aloud. The gifted reader finds this practice boring and the less able reader cannot keep his place. If the purpose is to have the children sense the rhythm pattern of a poem or there is some similar objective, then the procedure can be justified.

3. The teacher must be a good model for oral reading. A child's tendency to imitate the teacher's actions and performance is greater than many educators believe.

4. A receptive audience must be present when oral reading activities take place. The child who is reading must feel that he has a message to communicate and the children who are listening must feel that the information is important. Passive reading in a monotone in a class where some pupils are whispering, others are reading from other books, while still others are staring out the window is hardly an atmosphere for effective oral reading instruction.

Diagnosing Oral Reading Skills

As has been mentioned previously, a careful evaluation of the oral reading abilities of a given child may lend some valuable information toward helping him with silent reading deficiencies. There are at least two valuable standardized tests for measuring proficiency in oral reading alone—the *Gray Oral Reading Test* and the *Gilmore Oral Reading Test.* In addition, parts of the *Diagnostic Reading Scales,* the *Durrell Analysis of Reading Difficulty,* and the *Gates-McKillop Reading Test* are designed to provide data with regard to oral reading competency. (These tests are described in detail in a later chapter.)

One of the best procedures for evaluating a pupil's performance in oral reading is the use of an informal reading inventory along with careful day-to-day observation of his abilities in this area. The information regarding his strengths and limitations must be collected in an organized manner. A checklist such as the following should be used with each child.

ORAL READING CHECKLIST

Pupil's Name _____ Period Ending _____

	Unsatisfactory	Satisfactory	Outstanding
1. pronounces words correctly			
2. gives evidence of word meaning			
3. has a flexible and pleasing voice			
4. exhibits knowledge of proper phrasing of words			
5. uses variety in pitch, force, and speed			
6. shows sensitivity to audience reaction			
7. displays careful enunciation of words, particularly word endings			
8. appears relaxed when he reads			
9. gives impression of his own interpretation while reading			
10. shows desire to read many different kinds of material			

A careful analysis should be made of the results of the checklist at regular intervals and help should be given on an individual or small group basis to those pupils who have common limitations. Silent reading can be improved only after careful instruction has taken place in oral reading activities.

Examples of Profitable Lessons in Oral Reading

The resourceful, imaginative teacher can find many natural situations during any school day to promote good oral reading practices with her pupils. Several such situations are described in the following section.

1. Reading orally a story or play for entertainment purposes.

2. Reading the minutes of the last club meeting in order to inform the members of the actions which have been taken in the past.

3. Reading aloud a statement from a textbook or other source to substantiate or refute a remark made by the speaker or another classmate regarding a particular subject.

4. Reading aloud an important announcement which is of importance to all members of the audience.

5. Reading orally to others a particular part in a play which the class has composed.

6. Reading aloud to provide information which will help to solve a question which has arisen during a social studies or science class.

7. Reading orally a limerick in order to demonstrate rhythm in verse.

8. Reading aloud with the use of the tape recorder in order to listen to the actual mistakes made by the reader and thus serve to call attention to those oral reading areas which need further strengthening.

9. Reading a story or poem aloud in unison with a number of other pupils which serves to develop self-confidence and poise in an audience situation.

10. Reading a short story or poem to illustrate a lesson or moral.

In summary, oral reading must be promoted through natural yet meaningful situations which arise during the school day, not only in the formal reading period but during the content area lessons as well. By keeping in mind the principles and suggestions which have been mentioned, one can build a purposeful program of oral and silent reading activities.

DEVELOPING AN EFFECTIVE READING RATE

There is a natural concern on the part of teachers at the middle and upper grades with respect to the pupil who reads at a very slow rate. Teachers and pupils alike have become very conscious about this factor in reading since so much has been written about the importance of reading rate in popular and professional journals. Many commercial speed reading schools have developed in the larger cities of our country and fantastic claims have been made by the advertisers of some of these concerns. Unfortunately, many people have come to equate reading efficiency with reading rate. Many parents begin to fret about their child's reading rate in the middle and upper grades and secondary school.

Reading authorities discovered many years ago that a pupil cannot read any faster than he can *comprehend* the material. *Rate of reading must be geared to the reader's purpose*—in other words, if one is reading for details, slow, deliberate reading is needed; however, if getting the main idea is the principal objective, a faster skimming technique can be used. Too many pupils are guilty of attempting to read all materials at the same speed.

There are a number of causes for unduly slow reading. *First,* a gross deficiency may exist in the area of word attack skills. If the reader finds he has to use phonetic analysis to unlock words in place of sight word recognition or context clues, he, of course, will be forced to read at a slow rate. *Second,* the reader may not have any interest or purpose for reading. Reading assignments which are neither motivating nor challenging will cause the pupil to daydream and will result in a minimal level of comprehension in addition to a slow rate of reading. *Third,* the use of vocalization and finger pointing will necessarily impede a child's reading speed. When such manifestations are noticed they should be quietly dealt with in order to remove any further obstacle to growth in rate.

Suggestions for Improving Rate of Reading

This author has used many of the following principles and procedures successfully with pupils and has observed the use of most of them by master teachers at the intermediate and upper grade levels. The degree of success which one might expect from the use of any one technique or procedure will quite naturally depend on a given child's needs and temperament.

1. Mechanical pacers and various machines which control the rate of reading may be of some value to certain pupils. One should use caution in using such instruments on a wholesale basis. For example, pupils who have severe deficiencies in the area of word attack should have other kinds of training. For the child whose chief problem appears to be solely that of slow reading rate, a mechanical aid may serve profitably as a motivational device to increase rate. There appears to be, however, a considerable amount of debate with respect to how permanent the improvement is with the use of such aids.

2. The teacher must be sure that a purpose is given for each reading assignment. Each pupil should make the decision whether he should

skim the material, read moderately fast, or read at a slow rate. He should understand that he needs a reading "differential" with a number of reading gears for adjusting the speed of reading to the reading objective.

3. The use of timed reading practices may be profitable for those pupils reading at or above grade level. With this procedure, the teacher prepares a series of reading exercises which are of the same length and at similar levels with regard to readability. These three-minute exercises are given from three to five times a week and are followed by ten comprehension questions. The pupils are urged to increase the number of words read in succeeding exercises with at least a 70 per cent comprehension score on all exercises.

4. Each child should be asked to keep personal records of his rate progress from week to week when using the exercises described in the previous section. Attempting to better one's own previous score is the keenest kind of competition.

5. A continuous evaluation should be maintained with respect to the individual reading rates of the pupils. Standardized tests such as the *Diagnostic Reading Tests* and the *Sangren-Woody Reading Test* can be used for this purpose in addition to informal measures such as a subjective reading inventory.

In conclusion, one should not equate speed of reading with level of comprehension. A purpose should be given for reading a particular selection and the proper reading rate used which is practical for that purpose. Rate of reading can be increased without loss of comprehension if the suggestions that have been discussed are employed according to the individual needs of pupils.

FUNCTIONAL AND RECREATORY READING

All teachers at all grade levels have the responsibility for developing reading competency for all pupils in three areas: fundamental skill development, functional reading, and recreatory reading.

During the primary grades the main emphasis is placed on fundamental skill development in such areas as word attack skills and the various segments of comprehension. Beginning at the fourth grade level the child finds that he is required to read arithmetic and social studies assignments which require functional or work-type reading skills. He is expected to read to find the answer to a problem or a question.

While the child is expected to use functional or work-type reading skills proficiently at the middle and upper grade levels, the training and foundation for this skill must be started not later than the second or third grades.

The job of the teacher in the middle and upper grades is to provide suitable opportunities for each child to review and reinforce his functional reading skills. At no level can it be assumed that all pupils have completely mastered these skills.

As a part of the total reading curriculum, each pupil should be given training which will make him proficient in the following functional reading skill areas:

1. The use of the index, the key words, and how to find the name of a particular topic.

2. The ability to derive information from tables, figures, maps, and charts.

3. The use of different kinds of dictionaries.

4. The ability to profit from indications which might suggest whether a particular reference book may be of help to him for the purpose he has in mind. These aspects would include such items as the titles of the various chapters, the author and his background, the copyright date, and the title of the book.

5. The use of several kinds of encyclopedias, including skill in using the index, topic outlines, and other aspects of each volume.

6. The use of the library, including the various indexes and the card catalogue.

7. The use of the table of contents, particularly in non-reference books.

Instruction in the functional or work-type skills is not and should not be a hit-or-miss affair. The following principles should undergird all instructional procedures which are undertaken in this important area.

1. *Motivation for developing proficiency in the area of functional reading skills must always be present.* The teacher has the responsibility to arouse a felt need within the child to learn these skills. By demonstrating how knowledge about a particular area can be broadened through the use of the encyclopedia, the pupil will be lead to use this source and other sources for his own development and enrichment. Situations must be created in which the child feels the need for facility in a given skill.

2. *Opportunities must be afforded to make use of the work-type skills which have been learned.* If the use of the *World Almanac,* for example, has been explained to pupils, frequent meaningful situations must be provided in which the child will have need for the use of this aid. When all of the class members or a particular class member has a problem to solve, one should lead discussions in which the group will

decide which reference aid should be used. In addition to the use of incidental lessons, direct, sequential lessons must be provided to insure each child's competency in this important area.

An example of such a lesson might be one in which the teacher duplicates a series of questions which might be suggested by the pupils in relation to a social studies unit which is being studied. In each case the pupil is asked to tell precisely where he expects to find the requested information. The following might represent a copy of such a work sheet.

On the space which follows each question, indicate the name of the source where one might find the requested information. Keep in mind the names of all of the various sources such as the *World Book* and the *World Almanac* which we have recently studied.

1. What is the present capital of Brazil? _____

2. How does the population of Brazil and Argentina compare? _____
   _____

- 3. What is the meaning of the word, "fiesta"? _____

4. What is the chief cash crop of Brazil? _____

3. *Some provision must be made for the evaluation of work-type or functional reading skill development of individual pupils.* There are very few standardized tests which evaluate all of the work-type skills; however, the *Iowa Every-Pupil Tests of Basic Skills* contains appropriate sections which test skills in reading maps, use of references, index, dictionary, and alphabetizing (for 3–5) or reading graphs, charts, and tables (for 5–9). In addition to this test, teacher-made instruments can be constructed for evaluating these and other skills. Careful observation of the reading habits of each pupil in these areas should yield important information.

While much importance is given to each child having a high level of competency in the functional reading skill area, one must not overlook one of the *most* important products of any reading program—the desire of all children to read for fun and relaxation. The experiences of children can be widened greatly by their exploration of a large number of books in many different areas. "Whet" the desire of children to engage in recreatory reading by sponsoring book fairs, constructing bulletin boards which "advertise" new books, asking the school librarian to come to the classroom to give "teasers" about new books which have been recently catalogued, asking children to share exciting or humorous portions of some of the books which they have read recently with the remainder of the class, and displaying a selection of new library books on a specially designated table in the classroom.

THE TEACHER AND THE DEVELOPMENTAL READING PROGRAM

Since learning to read is a complex procedure, the reading program in any classroom should be constructed in such a manner that a careful balance is maintained among the important skill areas of word attack and comprehension as well as the skills in functional reading and the promotion of a desire to engage in recreatory reading.

The directed reading lesson constitutes the most important aspect of the reading program, especially for those school systems which make use of basal reading materials. While any reading lesson should be altered to care for the individual needs of each pupil according to his grade level and his strengths and limitations, the basic procedure is somewhat alike for all grade levels from three through eight. In the following section these procedures are described.

The *first* step in the development of the lesson should be that of *developing readiness* for the selection which is to be studied. At this stage, ask the children to relate any experiences which they may have had in light of the subject suggested by the title of the story. New vocabulary should be presented and a study of the pronunciation and meaning of the words should be undertaken. The purposes for reading the story should be given in order to improve comprehension skills. As an example, one might say to the pupils, "Let's read the story to find out why President Jefferson thought we ought to purchase the Louisiana Territory."

The *second* step of the lesson involves guided silent reading. During this period one should observe each child to discover reading limitations such as obvious word recognition difficulties, faulty habits such as finger pointing and vocalizations, and overall attitude with respect to the reading act. The importance of making sure that the reading material is on the child's instructional level cannot be overemphasized. If any child in the group cannot pronounce at least 95 per cent of the running words in the book or cannot comprehend at least 75 per cent of the material when reading silently, one must conclude that the reading selections are too difficult for him.

The *third* part of the reading lesson consists of the discussion of the selection and subsequent skill development. The discussion should be in terms of the questions which were posed at the beginning of the silent reading in order to build the various comprehension skill areas. Purposeful oral reading should take place during this stage. Suggestions with respect to the nature of these activities were described in an earlier part of this chapter. Practice exercises from the workbook may be assigned at this stage for those pupils who are in need of a given type of activity.

The *fourth* part of the reading lesson consists of the enrichment activities (sometimes called culminating activities). At this stage the pupils should be encouraged to read other stories and books which are on the same topic as the story just discussed. Some children may like to dramatize portions of the story for the rest of the pupils while others may wish to paint or draw scenes of some part of the story which was of great interest to them. As much correlation as possible should take place between the reading lesson activities and those in the areas of art, music, and social studies.

Complete suggestions which are appropriate for a particular story or selection will normally be found in the teacher's manual for the materials. In the absence of such aids, the preceding discussion should serve adequately as an outline for the development of a given lesson.

THE USE OF VARIOUS READING MATERIALS

For the vast majority of teachers, the reading materials for the developmental reading program consist of the basal readers, workbooks or practice books, manuals, accompanying tests, and charts of different kinds.

At the time of this writing, there is a materials explosion of fantastic proportions in progress. Numerous concerns are now publishing and constructing materials and devices which are supposed to help the teacher build a "complete" reading program. Unfortunately, many of these aids and devices have been compiled by persons with limited training in the area of reading instruction. Some overemphasize a certain phase of reading instruction (phonics, for example) and tend to give the impression that all other facets of the reading act are either unimportant or need little attention.

Evaluation and selection of materials for a reading program must be done in light of the objectives of the total reading program and the expressed demonstrated needs of the pupils. A list of several important supplemental reading aids and materials is included in the appendix of this volume. Secure sample copies of the items and examine them carefully. Ask the advice of the local or state reading supervisor or consultant regarding his or her views concerning the usefulness of a given aid. In any case, use a small quantity of the materials in a given situation before ordering large supplies of items which may be of little or no value for the pupils. Finally, one must also remember that no amount of materials will compensate for a poorly trained teacher. Excellent materials merely supplement the efforts of an excellent teacher who is aware of her pupils' needs.

Summary

A well-developed reading program at the intermediate and upper grade levels is based on carefully formulated objectives which serve to give each child sequential training in all aspects of reading.

Because of the wide range of reading abilities which are present at these levels, each teacher must devise some instructional plan such as a grouping procedure in order to better meet the needs of individual pupils. At the present time, research has not provided educators with an answer regarding the most efficient plan for any particular school situation.

Silent and oral reading are two very important segments of any reading lesson; however, one must remember to have children read material silently before asking them to read it orally. An audience situation should always prevail unless the reading is done for diagnostic purposes.

Rate of reading should be geared to the reader's purpose. If a pupil reads at an unduly slow rate, a number of practices can be employed to overcome the limitation, such as the use of mechanical devices and timed practice drills.

Since pupils are asked to search for information in many places in studying materials in the content areas, functional or work-type skills should be stressed at these grade levels. Recreatory reading should be encouraged by providing the child with a large number of interesting books on varying levels of difficulty.

The developmental reading lesson consists of four parts: building readiness for the selection, guiding silent reading, discussing the story and building skills, and providing for enrichment activities.

Selected References

1. Barbe, Walter B. *Educator's Guide to Personalized Reading Instruction.* Englewood Cliffs, New Jersey: Prentice-Hall, Inc., 1961. Chap. 8.
2. Bond, Guy L. and Tinker, Miles A. *Reading Difficulties: Their Diagnosis and Correction.* New York: Appleton-Century-Crofts, 1967. Chaps. 15, 16.
3. DeBoer, John and Dallman, Martha. *The Teaching of Reading.* New York: Holt, Rinehart and Winston, Inc., 1964. Chap. 15.
4. Dechant, Emerald. *Improving the Teaching of Reading.* Englewood Cliffs, New Jersey: Prentice-Hall, Inc., 1964. Chap. 9.
5. Gans, Roma. *Common Sense in Teaching Reading.* Indianapolis: The Bobbs-Merrill Company, Inc., 1963. Chap. 9.
6. Harris, Albert. *Effective Teaching of Reading.* New York: David McKay Company, Inc., 1962. Chaps. 5, 6, 7.
7. Heilman, Arthur. *Principles and Practices of Teaching Reading.* Columbus: Charles E. Merrill Books, Inc., 1967. Chap. 8.
8. McKim, Margaret and Caskey, Helen. *Guiding Growth in Reading.* New York: The Macmillan Company, 1963. Chaps. 10, 11, 12.
9. Ramsey, Wallace Z. *Organizing for Individual Differences.* Perspectives In Reading No. 9, Newark, Delaware: International Reading Association, 1968.
10. Russell, David. *Children Learn to Read.* Waltham, Massachusetts: Blaisdell Publishing Company, 1961. Chap. 8.

11. Smith, Henry P. and Dechant, Emerald. *Psychology in Teaching Reading.* Englewood Cliffs, New Jersey: Prentice-Hall, Inc., 1961. Chap. 14.
12. Smith, Nila B. *Reading Instruction for Today's Children.* Englewood Cliffs, New Jersey: Prentice-Hall, Inc., 1963. Chaps. 6, 7, 11.
13. Witty, Paul A., Freeland, Alma Moore, and Grotberg, Edith H. *The Teaching of Reading.* Boston: D. C. Heath and Company, 1966. Chap. 10.

5

Developing Word–Attack Skills

The most vital and significant aspect of learning to read is the recognition of words. There are a number of tools which may be used to unlock words in different situations. Accordingly, pupils must be given sequential instruction at the various grade levels in the use of context clues, phonetic and structural analysis principles, picture clues, configuration aids, and the dictionary. In order to insure maximum reading growth for each child, an on-going program of evaluation in this important area is necessary.

This chapter is designed to investigate the place of word-attack skills in the reading program; explore the nature and importance of each of the various word analysis tools; reveal the steps involved in the effective development of these techniques; and provide a description of some of the commercial and teacher-made materials which can be used in this vital area.

THE PLACE OF WORD-ATTACK SKILLS
IN THE READING PROGRAM

Throughout educational history, the one area of reading instruction which has caused the most controversy has been that of the procedures used for the teaching of word-attack skills. The literature reveals that there have been many movements and crossmovements regarding this significant subject, and during the last several decades there has been an interesting rise and fall of different trends in this area. The advantages and limitations of the "look-say" and phonetic approaches have been discussed at some length in the professional journals and in workshops. The continuing controversy leaves teachers honestly confused about which emphasis should be stressed in an effective word-attack program.

The heart of the reading act is that of word perception. There is no practical need for one to become excited about teaching the different comprehension skill strands if the child cannot unlock words. Word-attack skills have one expressed purpose in the complex task of learning to read— to help the pupil to pronounce an unknown word and relate it with a known word which is a part of his listening and/or speaking vocabulary. All reading authorities recognize the need for teaching word-attack skills. The real query is, "Which method shall I use for a particular child in a particular context at a particular time?" Children learn at different rates and come from different backgrounds and have had many different kinds of experiences; it is, therefore, extremely difficult to manufacture a formula or procedure which will absolutely insure that all children will be able to unlock all words which confront them.

One of the important principles which one should keep in mind in word-attack skill development is that *all* teachers are responsible for this area of instruction. The major emphasis is given most surely at the primary grade level, but if a given pupil is not provided instruction in the higher skills of structural analysis by the intermediate and upper grade teachers, then he will be shortchanged as an adult reader. A constant reteaching and reviewing of even the most elementary phonetic generalizations is vitally necessary in the higher grades; in fact, one could say that the sixth grade teacher should know and understand the process of word-attack development better than any other teacher in a particular elementary school. Educators know that repetition is necessary for the concrete learning of any skill, and the skill involved in unlocking words is certainly no exception.

In the typical basal reading materials program, the pupils are introduced to different skills in the primary grades, and for a number of reasons the intermediate teachers are expected to observe carefully those children who need to be reintroduced to a skill. The administration of both standardized and teacher-made tests may be necessary for a complete analysis which will provide the teacher with the exact nature of a given child's difficulty and the extent of limitation in any particular area. After these procedures are accomplished, help groups should be formed within the class and disbanded after each of the group members has reached a satisfactory level of accomplishment in a particular area of word-attack skills. Materials which should be used with these groups would include workbooks, special practice books, teacher-made materials, and commercial and teacher-made games of different types. The message to the middle and upper grade teacher is clear: continue the sequential development of word-attack skills and reteach those which are clearly not at a satisfactory level.

DIFFERENT WORD ANALYSIS TOOLS WHICH MAY BE USED TO UNLOCK WORDS

A carpenter needs a variety of tools to build a house. The use of a single tool such as a claw hammer or a saw is not sufficient for all situations. The young child should similarly be equipped with a number of techniques for approaching and pronouncing new words. With most words he will employ the use of several tools—with others the use of one or two tools may be quite sufficient. He may, for example, ask his friend to pronounce a word, and at the same time he will take note of its use in that particular context; then he will attempt to remember the word the next time he sees it in a similar context. The very young child may be helped to analyze a word by taking note of its shape and general feature (this technique, however, should be used to a very limited degree as explained later in this chapter). Since the English language is approximately 86 per cent phonetic, he may wish to make use of some phonetic generalization (not rule) which he has learned. A careful dissection of the word into its component parts—the roots, prefixes, suffixes, and inflectional endings—may give important clues to the pronunciation and meaning of a given word. The dictionary is an important tool for use in word perception development as early as the second grade. The picture dictionary helps the child to define the word and to associate a picture with a word and to further strengthen the meaning of the word in his mind. Picture clues may be of some aid to the child in certain situations.

The good reader makes use of all of the techniques described previously. Seldom will a pupil employ the use of a single tool since several word-attack skills are generally used simultaneously. He is able to use these skills in combination because he has a complete understanding of all of them singularly. A child who is limited in any one of the important areas of word-attack will have much difficulty at a later date in the total reading situation.

In the following section, the six most important word-attack skills are described and are accompanied by practical teaching suggestions for developing each skill. They are presented in the following order: configuration clues, context clues, phonetic analysis, structural analysis, sight words, and the dictionary.

CONFIGURATION CLUES

The development of the ability to use word-form or configuration clues is one of the very first procedures in word recognition training. Since many of the basic sight words are often recognized by their general shape or by some other particular detail, pupils should be taught to analyze words carefully by such identifying aspects as length, regularity or irregularity of form, double letters, height of letters, and letters which drop below the line of print.

This procedure loses much of its effectiveness as the child adds words to his sight vocabulary. A large number of words look very much alike and the greater number of words that are added to the sight vocabulary, the more difficult it becomes to differentiate one from another on the basis of their configuration alone.

Much difficulty is encountered in trying to determine the point at which configuration clues fail, and other more analytical clues should be employed. Many persons recognize thousands of words from their particular characteristics, especially when the words are seen or heard frequently.

The use of configuration clues can be effective if the number of words in the child's reading vocabulary is small. An example of such an exercise follows:

I want to go see the monkey.
|to| |go| |monkey|

In the first stages of developing a sight vocabulary, the child will have little trouble in noticing the differences between such words as "to" and "grandmother" since one is very short word and the other is relatively long. When he sees words which look alike ("horse" and "house," "see" and "saw," "he" and "me"), it is obvious that difficulties will arise. For this particular situation, the pupil must switch to the use of context clues.

The teacher can help the child make use of configuration clues by employing any one or more of the following exercises:

1. Matching short phrases in a list with those found in context.
2. Matching words found in print in the basal reader with those printed on the greenboard by the teacher.
3. Matching the lower case initial-letter form of a word with the capitalized form of a word.

The use of configuration clues or any other recognition technique is not complete until the pupil has made use of the word in spoken language, associated the symbol with the spoken word, and made use of it in a context which is sensible and meaningful.

CONTEXT CLUES

One of the most useful of the word-attack skills is that of the employment of context clues. The most efficient reader at all levels cannot afford the time to carefully analyze each word in detail. The use of context clues means studying the words which are known in the immediate vicinity of the unknown word in order to get an idea that will help the pupil discover what the unfamiliar word is.

One should remember, however, that the use of this technique is valuable only if the unknown word is a part of the reader's hearing or speaking vocabulary. If the word is not part of his vocabulary, the use of other word-attack skills is necessary to check his estimate of what the word might be. The primary teacher should not make the error of insisting that children make heavy or inappropriate use of the context clue method. One must remember that the use of this procedure requires close figure study along with the employment of the other common word-attack skills.

Beginning readers should be taught to use context clues as early as possible in the reading instruction program. Remember that the procedure is principally one of experimentation. Since in many instances more than one word properly fits the context, the sole employment of context clues sometimes is the cause of errors in word perception. For this reason it is vital to encourage the pupils to use several methods of word-attack along with context clues in order to narrow the possibility of a mistake on the first trial.

PHONETIC ANALYSIS

Since a detailed discussion with respect to the place and importance of phonics is included in a later portion of this chapter, a brief résumé of this word-attack approach will suffice at this point.

On the first day of school, Kirk, Claudine, Annabelle, and the twenty-five or so other eager-to-learn first graders come marching into the first grade classroom. In their minds, school means just one thing to them— "I'm going to read!" They have heard and observed that being able to read opens the doorway to a new avenue of adventure and knowledge. The teacher's job is to teach all of these very different children to learn to read.

One of the techniques which should be used to help these pupils to gain success in reading will most certainly be that of phonetic analysis. Despite some popular misconceptions to the contrary, most teachers "worth their salt" have from the beginning of modern educational history recognized that a high percentage of the words in the English language are highly regular in a phonetic sense and have provided their children with the appropriate phonetic training to unlock words. A child without knowledge of phonic skills is as handicapped as a mechanic without wrenches.

Phonetic analysis serves these important goals in a well-balanced reading program:

1. Unquestionably gives the child a very important aid for recognizing words that he has met on previous occasions.

2. Gives the pupil a tool for identifying new and unfamiliar words.

3. Helps to provide the pupil with the ability to enunciate clearly and pronounce each word properly.

4. Provides the pupil with a valuable aid to spelling since it trains him to hear sounds more accurately.

The individual needs of each child should be carefully considered since two of the common pitfalls in phonics instruction are those of over-emphasis or underemphasis. Some students require very little phonics instruction; others require intensive instruction on an individual or small group basis. The principal responsibility of the teacher is to carefully determine the individual differences in levels of achievement and the individual instructional needs to determine properly the nature of the phonics instruction needed for each pupil.

STRUCTURAL ANALYSIS

Analyzing words in terms of their morphemes or meaning units is known as structural analysis. For instance, in the word "unmatched", when analyzed structurally, one notes the prefix *un*, the root word *match,* and the suffix *ed*. If the child can pronounce a large number of root words, he then, by adding various suffixes and prefixes, is able to pronounce many additional words.

The importance of developing proficiency in structural analysis cannot be overstressed when one analyzes the vocabulary that the intermediate and upper grade child meets in typical social studies and science books. In ten pages of a social studies book it is not at all uncommon to find as many as 200 polysyllabic words. As many as 75 of these words might have inflectional endings, and another 150 might have suffixes; many of these words will have prefixes as well. In fact, there are few polysyllabic words which are not compounds or are without a prefix, suffix, or an inflectional ending.

One of the very first steps in learning the principles of structural analysis (usually in the first grade) is to recognize the inflectional endings of the language such as *s, es, ed, er,* and *ing*. Words in many first and second grade basal readers (such as "buys," "fishes," "walked," "baker," "walking") contain root words and inflectional endings. The first grade teacher should acquaint the children with compound words and teach them to divide compound words into two words such as *classroom, class room; today, to day;* and *fireman, fire man.* A word of caution is necessary with respect to this technique. Sometimes a combination of letters that would in isolation make a word by itself is neither a syllable nor a meaning unit when this combination of letters appears in a long word. Finding "map" in *maple* is misleading to the pupil and may cause him to be distrustful of the procedure in legitimate circumstances.

With respect to inflectional endings and root words, the child should be taught to have a thorough understanding of the following principles:

1. Many words are formed by adding inflectional endings with no change in the root word: lick*ed,* boy*s,* ask*ing,* watch*es.*

2. If the root words end in the final *e,* the *e* is dropped when an ending that begins with a vowel is added. (mak*e,* making).

3. If a syllable or root word ends in a single consonant preceded by a vowel, the consonant may often be doubled when an ending is added: (step, stepped; pet, petting).

4. Words ending in "f" or "fe" usually form their plurals by changing the "f" to a "v" and adding the plural endings: (knives, scarves).

5. When a word ends with "y", preceded by a consonant, the "y" is usually changed to an "i" before an ending is added: (babies, emptied). If the "y" is preceded by a vowel, there is no change in the root word when an ending is added: (annoys, deployed).

At about the fourth grade level, pupils discover dozens of polysyllabic words which cannot seemingly be unlocked by the more common word recognition techniques. Accordingly, a fourth grade teacher must introduce a number of syllabication principles for dealing with the longer words. The child is made aware of the place of accent by carefully designed listening exercises in which such factors are stressed as primary accent, secondary accent, and unaccented syllables; the pupil's attention is directed to the symbols which are used to denote primary and secondary accent (') in source books. One should not think of these facets as being separate teaching steps but rather a meaningful combination of all of them in order that the child may see the correct relationship among them. The previous matter should be approached from the point of view that they are helpful generalizations rather than rules, since there are a large number of exceptions.

A thorough understanding of the principles of syllabication is important to careful spelling, effective speaking, and correct writing patterns. When the syllabication principles are used with other accepted word recognition techniques, the child has taken a giant step toward reading success.

Syllabication Principles To Be Taught

A limited number of syllabication principles should be learned and employed by the elementary school pupil. The most valuable of these are as follows:

1. Every syllable has one vowel sound.

2. If a word contains a prefix and a root word, the word is usually divided between these two meaning units.

3. If the first vowel letter in a word is followed by two consonant letters, the first syllable usually ends with the first of two consonants.

4. If the first vowel letter (or letters) in a word is followed by a single consonant letter, the consonant usually begins the second syllable.

5. When the first vowel element is followed by a two-letter consonant symbol (sh, th), this symbol is not usually broken when the word is divided into syllables and may go with either syllable.

6. When the first vowel element of a word is followed by a consonant blend, the blend often begins the second syllable. (cy clone)

Suggestions For Teaching Structural Analysis

In summary, keep the following statements in mind in teaching structural analysis as a word-attack tool:

1. *Don't stress the procedure of finding small words or word parts in longer words.* Occasionally, in the case of compound words, it is perfectly justifiable to look for the two words which constitute a true compound word. This procedure may prove hazardous, however, if the reader makes the decision that the small words in *breakfast* are *fast* and *break*.

2. *Help the child analyze "strange" words in a meaningful context rather than in an isolated list.* Since meaningful word-attack is based on the use of several approaches, the reader may discover that context clues provide an important help in recognizing and understanding unfamiliar words.

3. *The child should recognize that other word-attack skills may be more suitable than structural analysis on certain occasions.* Sometimes a word can be recognized much quicker through the use of context clues and configuration clues—if so, these should be used in place of structural analysis. A pupil should never be given the impression that it is necessary to recognize all words by finding meaning units. The proper approach is one which makes use of several word-attack skills in combination.

4. *Structural analysis generalizations should be developed inductively.* The generalizations (not rules) should not be memorized "coldly" by the child. Situations should be developed which are illustrative of a generalization being emphasized. For instance, if the words "ladder" and "matter" were placed on the greenboard (along with other similar words), one would expect the pupils to discover the generalization

that when the first vowel letter in a word is followed by two consonant letters, the first syllable usually ends with the first of the two consonants.

5. *Structural analysis must be taught in a sequential manner and should never be left to chance.* In a basal program, the authors of the teachers' manuals clearly indicate in nearly every instance the generalizations which should be developed at the various levels. In using a program other than a basal materials approach, the use of a reference such as Dr. William S. Gray's *On Their Own in Reading* (Scott, Foresman, 1960) should prove helpful in this regard.

Sample Lesson Plans in Structural Analysis

The following section contains a sample of some of the lessons which serve to strengthen the child's skills in the area of structural analysis:

A. Several words known to the children should be written on the board or a piece of oaktag and then used in meaningful oral sentences. As an example, the words *eat, weak, faith,* and *slight* might be used. Write *eating, weakly, unfaithful,* and *slightly* on the board or paper. The child should be asked to find the root words and to use the new words in sentences either orally or in writing.

B. At the beginning of the second grade, attention should be given to the use and presence of compound words in the English language. Carefully chosen words such as *classroom, inside, grandmother, rainstorm* and *something* should be used. The pupil should be asked to find the two smaller words in each of the compound words. Caution should be exercised and emphasized since some words such as *maple* and *breakfast* would not fit into the general lesson objective.

C. At the first grade level, the child meets few if any words with prefixes or suffixes; however, at the second grade level the child typically encounters many such words. To emphasize the meaning of such words, one might write several sentences on the greenboard which contain certain known words. The children should be asked to read the sentences both silently and orally and to underline the known words. As a meaningful exercise, the pupils might be asked to recopy the sentences, adding an affix to the words so that the meaning of the words are changed. An example might be: "The floors were clean." The alert child should change the sentence so it reads: "The floors were unclean."

D. Numerous cards can be made on which affixes of different kinds have been printed. With these cards in the hands of the pupils, the children are shown various cards on which root words have been printed. A child who holds a card with appropriate affixes for a given root word makes this fact known by raising his or her hand and recording the newly formed word on a piece of paper.

E. The awareness of the different syllables should be stressed at the second and third grade levels. As certain two-syllable words such as *asleep* and *people* are pronounced, the child should either write or say the syllables heard. At a later time, you can proceed to three- and four-syllable words, using the same teaching procedure as with the two-syllable words.

THE USE OF SIGHT WORDS AS A WORD RECOGNITION TOOL

Most authors of basal materials recommend that the primary teacher build a basic stock of approximately 50 to 100 sight words with the children. Provision is made in the story content for frequent repetition of the words. Since a meaningful approach to learning is first the analysis of the whole and then its parts, it would appear that this procedure is based on sound reasoning. Dr. Dolch built a list of 220 words which he felt all children leaving the third grade should know by sight, since these words constitute approximately 65 per cent of the running words of the typical primary readers. Even though the list was constituted many years ago, it is just as usable today as it was at that time.

With the sight word approach the child is given the impression that he is gaining early success in reading. The length of time needed to perform the reading act after phonetic and structural analysis techniques are developed is too long for many children. The eager learner has the desire to "read" from the first day of school.

Some principles should be remembered in teaching the basic stock of sight words. First, the teaching of basic phonetic generalizations should be undertaken while the basic stock of sight words is being developed. Second, the number of unfamiliar words presented at one time should be relatively small depending on the maturity and interest of the pupils. The presentation of a large number of words tends to discourage even the most enthusiastic child. Third, numerous situations should be presented which will force the child to pronounce the newly-learned word.

THE DICTIONARY AS A WORD PERCEPTION TOOL

The proper use of a good dictionary can be an important tool in developing the pronunciation and meaning of various words. The development of the dictionary habit is hinged upon a well-organized program of instruction carried out under the direction of a skilled teacher. Picture dictionaries are used quite frequently at the second grade level, and regular classroom dictionaries are used for the first time no later than the third or early fourth grade.

The introduction to the use of the dictionary should certainly be gradual, and lesson plans for the sequential development of the plans should be devised with much care. Dictionaries should be made available to each individual child at all times; in fact, it is highly desirable for each student to have a dictionary of his own. At the present moment several companies have produced both pupil and teacher editions.

A number of factors with regard to the dictionary should be stressed with the pupils. The pupils should be taught to make the proper use of such facets as guide words, pronunciation keys, and diacritical and accent marks.

In summary, the child's use of the dictionary should not be left to chance. Direct, sequential development of dictionary skills is necessary. This important tool can help the child immeasurably in his task of mastering the multitude of new words which he encounters.

AN OUTLINE OF THE SEQUENTIAL DEVELOPMENT OF WORD-ATTACK SKILLS

The exact sequence for the development of word-attack skills is, of course, a debatable matter. Each editor of the various basal material programs has a definite organization to follow to insure sequential development in this area. The following outline is a general statement of a program which might be followed in any particular school system.

1. *Readiness level.* Readiness activities which stress auditory and visual discrimination: listening to sounds—high and low, soft and loud; listening to follow directions; telling a simple story in sequence; noting and reproducing sounds made by other children and the teacher; matching letters and words.

2. *Preprimer level.* Reinforcement of readiness activities; developing a basic stock of forty to fifty words; listening to and producing various initial consonant sounds; insight into the construction of simple compound words such as "play" and "ground" in the word "playground"; noting words which rhyme; seeing the relationship between auditory and visual symbols with particular objects and pictures.

3. *Primer level.* Attention to visual differences in words (configuration); matching words and syllables with similar consonant sounds; recognizing various prefix and suffix forms such as "un", "non", "s", "ed", and "ing"; reciting and constructing short poems which have rhyming words; addition of forty to fifty additional words to the basic stock of sight words.

4. *First-grade level.* Association of one consonant sound with double consonant letters at the end of a word (bell, toss) and with the two-letter symbols "wh", "th", and similar combinations; introduction of consonant blends (tr, gr, gl, for example); substitution of consonant blends at the beginning of a word to form a new word in a story; knowledge of the concept of a root word as a meaning unit; attention

to similar, but different words (were and wear, then and when, for example).

5. *Second-grade level.* Review of the word analysis procedures taught at the previous level; attacking new words by blending with initial consonants; developing consonant sound relationships such as a consonant letter which represents more than one sound (c in cost and cell); two consonant letters may stand for one sound (the two "ll's" in mill); specific knowledge concerning long and short vowel sounds (the long "a" in gate; the short "a" in apple); identification and understanding of consonant digraphs (ch, sh, th, wh, for example); knowledge and use of open and closed syllables (fo, bo, re, pes, rud, sof, for example); understanding of the place of the final "e" principle (safe, mite); introduction of inflectional endings such as "es" and "est"; acquaintance with the principle of changing the final "y" to "i" in a word (baby, babies); and recognition of words which are contractions.

6. *Third-grade level.* Applying word-analysis techniques to multisyllable words; study and employment of vowel digraphs, (such as *ea* in meat; *ai* in rain; *oa* in boat); diphthongs (*oi* in oil; *oy* in boy; *ou* in out, for example); and understanding of hard and soft sounds of "c" and "g"; study of the contractions and possessives that drop more than one letter; study of the alphabet preparatory to dictionary study; instruction in the application of the various syllabication principles; meaning of accents in syllables.

7. *Fourth-grade level.* Refining skill in the use of a number of word perception skills in combination; review and necessary reteaching of skills introduced at the preceding levels; extensive use of the dictionary and all of its different parts; intensive study of synonyms, antonyms, and homonyms, and multiple word meanings; use of phonetic analysis in identifying words of three or more syllables; further introduction to prefixes and suffixes and their use as meaning units.

8. *Fifth- through twelfth-grade level.* Review and reteaching of any of the skills outlined at the lower grade levels; instruction in the area of structural analysis dealing with three or more syllable words; use of unabridged dictionary and other specialized aids; evaluating and planning each child's program in word recognition on the basis of individual need.

PLACE AND IMPORTANCE OF PHONICS IN THE SEQUENTIAL DEVELOPMENT OF WORD-ATTACK SKILLS

No area of the curriculum has undergone more experimentation than that of reading, and yet no field finds educators in less agreement regarding proper teaching approaches. Quite often one finds a writer who proposes what he considers the best method and eliminates all other procedures regardless of their proven advantages. Some conclusions are based on valid research studies, some are gained from limited observation, and others are the result of opinion. With such diversified views presented in educational journals, many classroom teachers are honestly confused. One problem awaiting adequate solution is the role of phonics in the teaching of reading. Practically all educators admit this is a controversial subject—not from the point of view that is in an important word-attack skill, but rather the degree of emphasis it should receive in the overall instructional program.

The controversy has a lengthy history and has been prominent since the study of the sounds of words was first considered in reading instruction. Due to several influences, the use of phonics in teaching reading was in evidence from earliest times, but approval of the procedure did not appear until the end of the nineteenth century.

Beginning around 1890 and continuing for a period of approximately thirty-five years, the chief method of word-attack emphasized in American schools was the synthetic phonics approach. Sounds of the various letters were stressed, and children were asked to drill on isolated lists of sounds such as "ma," "re," and "li." The end product of the approach was a very mechanical approach to reading, and word-calling without an emphasis on meaning was the rule of the day. Efficiency in reading was equated with a child's ability to pronounce the words in the reader or story book. The questionable practice of "finding little words in big words" was advocated.

In the early 1920's many educators came to believe that phonics instruction was unsound as a word-perception tool, and accordingly the technique was entirely eliminated in the reading curriculum of many schools. For a period of approximately twenty years, phonics instruction was not included in the lesson plans of many teachers. From the early 1940's to the present date, most eminent reading authorities believe that phonetic analysis is indeed one of the most important skills which the child should possess and have accordingly given such instruction a place in the word-attack program.

At the time this book is being printed, the following statements appear to reflect the current thinking of most reading authorities with respect to the place of phonetic instruction in the total reading program:

1. Since the English language is approximately 86 per cent regular, phonetically, the use of this technique is very important—perhaps the most significant of the word-attack skills. There is no place for an "all or nothing" debate regarding the topic.

2. Since many words cannot be unlocked by phonetic methods, the teacher must provide the pupils with other methods such as structural analysis, context clues, configuration clues, and picture clues. The alert pupil employs these procedures in combination.

3. The basis for all instruction in the area of phonics is competence in discriminating between various speech sounds and printed letters.

4. The concept should be established with the pupils that phonic principles are called "generalizations" and *not* "rules", since many of the principles have widely varying degrees of utility in actual practice.

5. Phonic principles which are necessary for a child to become an efficient reader should be developed sequentially from the primary grades through the high school levels.

6. Phonic generalizations should be taught from the inductive approach, not the deductive approach. For such principles to be meaningful, the child must "discover" the reason and not be told the reason.

7. Those generalizations which have very limited application should not be taught by the phonics method. These words could be taught from the sight word approach.

8. It is vitally important for all teachers to know the complete sequence of phonetic generalizations to be taught. A given teacher should heed the admonition to take the child where "she finds him." One could properly say that upper grade teachers should have even a greater knowledge of the skills in this area than the primary teacher. (This is unfortunately not true in the vast majority of the cases.)

9. A quality phonics program makes provision for differentiated instruction. Not all pupils need the same amount of instruction in this area. It is a tragic waste of time to subject alert, gifted pupils to needless drill on principles which are obviously designed for those at remedial levels.

10. Instruction in phonics should be a part of the developmental reading period and not an isolated activity in the other half of the school day. Such "cold" teaching of unrelated principles leads ultimately to boredom and meaningless drill for many pupils.

11. Since most editors of basal materials make adequate provision for training in phonetic analysis, there is little justification for separate, distinct materials for this purpose except for use with disabled readers.

STEPS IN PHONICS INSTRUCTION

One of the important considerations in phonics instruction is that of the sequential development of phonetic generalizations which are important to the child in unlocking words at the various grade levels. One must realize that there is no one set pattern for the development of such skills; however, many authorities agree on a general outline of the instructional procedures.

The following outline is a framework of an instructional pattern which might be used for the construction of such skills:

1. Auditory and visual discrimination of words and sounds
2. Initial consonant sounds
3. Final consonant sounds
4. Consonant blends and digraphs
5. Short and long vowel sounds
6. Final "e" principle
7. Open and closed syllables
8. Irregular and silent consonants
9. "R", "l", and "w" controllers
10. Dipthongs
11. Vowel and consonant digraphs
12. Instruction in short and long vowel sounds in combination
13. Syllabication principles
14. Generalizations with respect to prefixes and suffixes
15. Use and importance of compound words
16. The meaning of primary and secondary accent

The outline listed above is merely a general design. It is not one of the objectives of this volume to outline in detail all of the minute steps under each of the broad topics. The reader should study the teaching guides which accompany a particular basal material or consult volumes by Gray, Heilman, Cordts, and others which are mentioned in the reference section of this chapter.

GENERAL PRINCIPLES FOR TEACHING WORD-ATTACK SKILLS

In summary, each teacher should keep in mind that there are certain principles which should be remembered in teaching the word-attack skills:

1. All words should be taught in a contextual situation. Words may be taught in isolation only when the repetition of known segments of the word will result in learning new words.

2. The skills and abilities necessary for efficient word-attack must be taught in sequential order.

3. Children differ considerably in the amount of training or emphasis which may be needed for a particular skill. A fourth grade pupil, for instance, may need a complete reteaching of most of the basic skills of phonetic and structural analysis while another child in the same room may be very efficient with respect to these skills.

4. Generalizations should be taught from the inductive, *not* deductive, point of view. When children discover for themselves the rationale for a particular principle, a meaningful mind set is more apt to result.

5. Frequent review of individual word-attack skills in both group and individual situations is absolutely necessary. The influence of forgetting is more powerful than one realizes. "Solid" learning takes place through much repetition in meaningful situations.

6. There is no one method or approach to word perception skills which is so superior to all other methods that it should be used on an exclusive basis. The efficient reader uses a combination of procedures in unlocking words.

7. The needs of the pupils should dictate the appropriateness of a particular method at any particular time.

8. The teacher should make use of a wide variety of materials in word recognition instruction.

COMMERCIAL MATERIALS FOR DEVELOPING WORD PERCEPTION SKILLS

Although there are a number of commercial materials available for developing the skills mentioned in the previous section, one should not underestimate his or her own ability to produce meaningful exercises for the precise purposes which might be sought for a particular child. Commercial materials are helpful sources of material for general needs; however, only those exercises which are meaningful to the child and meet a particular need should be selected. There is little justification for all pupils being forced to complete every page of every practice book, regardless of need.

The following list of commercial materials are those known to this author and are being used by varying numbers of school systems:

Phonic Systems

1. *Phonovisual Method* by Lucille D. Schoolfield and Josephine B. Timberlake (Phonovisual Products Company). This series consists of a manual, charts illustrating various vowels and consonant sounds, a workbook for students, and a phonograph record. A group of charts has been devised for use by individual pupils.

2. *Reading with Phonics* by Julie Hay and Charles E. Wingo (J. B. Lippincott Co.). A hardback book and three workbooks are provided for each pupil in addition to a teacher's manual. The use of practice exercises involving consonant-vowel combinations provides reinforcement and reteaching of these skills.

Miscellaneous Commercial Aids*

1. *Phonics We Use* (Lyons & Carnahan) is a series of workbooks designed for children reading at grade levels one through six. Books A and B are at the first grade level, Book C is at the second grade level, Book D is third grade level, Book E is fourth grade level, Book F is fifth grade level, and Book G is sixth grade level. There is also a set of ten reading games which can be used with the materials.

2. *Reading Essentials Series* (Steck-Vaughn Company) is designed for pupils reading at any reading level from one through eight. Even though the exercises are designed to give practice in a number of skills, word-analysis skills are emphasized. There are a number of games including *Phono Wheels* and *Phrase-O-Game* which can be used.

3. *Dolch Play-Way Learning Games* (Garrard Press) constitutes a series of interesting games for use with children who are deficient in word-recognition skills. Among the games are BASIC SIGHT VOCABULARY CARDS, POPPER WORDS, GROUP WORD TEACHING GAME, SENTENCE GAME, CONSONANT LOTTO, VOWEL LOTTO, GROUP SOUNDING GAME, and SYLLABLE SOLITAIRE.

4. *Linguistic Block Series* (Scott, Foresman & Company) is designed to help children gain an awareness of the structure of our language and to add to their basic stock of sight words. Included in the series are THE FIRST ROLLING READER (Primer level); THE SECOND ROLLING READER (Book one level); THE THIRD ROLLING READER (Book 2/1 level); ROLLING PHONICS-VOWELS (for practice in associating vowel sounds with letters and in developing first recognition of major sound-spelling patterns); ROLLING PHONICS-CONSONANTS (for practice in adding and substituting initial consonants and consonant blends).

5. *Phonic Key Cards* (McCormick-Mathers Publishing Company) are pictured key cards which are designed to accompany the workbooks of the BUILDING READING SKILLS SERIES. They can be used when teaching the sounds of vowels, blends, consonants, digraphs, and diphthongs.

6. *Webster Word Wheels* (Webster Division, McGraw-Hill Book Company) (By Dr. William Kottmeyer of St. Louis) is designed to assist pupils in the middle and upper grades in the learning of the beginning blends, prefixes, and suffixes. These are useful in both developmental and remedial programs.

* Addresses for the various publishers can be found in Appendix D.

7. *The Macmillan Reading Spectrum* (The Macmillan Company) consists of two programs: THE SPECTRUM OF SKILLS and THE SPECTRUM OF BOOKS. The SKILLS program consists of six skills booklets in word analysis, six in vocabulary, and six in comprehension. The materials are very useful for children in the intermediate and junior high levels and are designed to individualize reading for those enrolled in either developmental or remedial programs.

8. *Word Games* is one of the boxed SRA READING LABORATORY SERIES (Science Research Associates) and is constructed for use in conjunction with the primary READING LABORATORY 1. The many word games provide a means for the reinforcement of phonics instruction. The Teacher's Handbook is an invaluable source of information for teachers with respect to the games which should be used with pupils who display certain deficiencies in the area of word analysis.

9. *The Webster Classroom Reading Clinic* (Webster Division, McGraw-Hill Book Company) is a box of materials for use with those pupils who need supplementary help in word analysis, comprehension, and spelling. The components of the set consist of the MAGIC WORLD OF DR. SPELLO, THE NEW WEBSTER WORD WHEELS, BASIC SIGHT VOCABULARY CARDS, GROUP WORD TEACHING GAME, THE READING SKILL CARDS, and EVERYREADERS (a series of ten readers which contain some of the world's favorite books which are adapted so that no book exceeds the fourth grade level in reading difficulty, yet is of high interest for the children ten through eighteen). THE TEACHER'S GUIDE FOR REMEDIAL READING accompanies the materials.

Summary

Developing independence in word recognition is one of the most important goals of reading instruction—in fact, since this skill is the center of the reading act, one might well say that it is the most important goal. A child who is inefficient in word perception skills cannot expect to be efficient in the area of comprehension.

The child should be taught to make use of any one of several methods for word-attack: phonetic analysis, structural analysis, use of context clues, picture clues, configuration clues, sight words, and the use of the dictionary. For any one word, the pupils make use of a combination of tools. One should give appropriate emphasis to all of these techniques and not give the child the idea that there is only one way to unlock words.

A number of materials have been described which are useful to the teacher in her instructional program. A careful examination of the materials should be made to determine if the exercises present materials and information which will serve the needs of the pupils in a particular group.

An analysis of the level of each child's achievement in each of the skill areas should be made periodically. Appropriate help groups should be established for those pupils who need additional training in the various areas of word perception.

Selected References

1. Artley, A. Sterl, "Controversial Issues Relating to Word Perception," *Reading Teacher,* VIII (April, 1955), 196–99.
2. Barbe, Walter B. *Educator's Guide to Personalized Reading Instruction.* Englewood Cliffs, New Jersey: Prentice-Hall, Inc., 1961, Chaps. 7 and 8.
3. Bear, David E., "Phonics for First Grade: A Comparison of Two Methods", *Elementary School Journal, LIX* (April, 1959), 394–402.
4. Bloomer, Richard H., "An Investigation of an Experimental First Grade Phonics Program," *Journal of Educational Research,* LIII (January, 1960), 188–93.
5. Bond, Guy L. and Wagner, Eva Bond. *Teaching the Child to Read.* (4th ed.) New York: The Macmillan Company, 1966. Chap. 8.
6. Cordts, Anna D. *Phonics for the Reading Teacher.* New York: Holt, Rinehart and Winston, Inc., 1965.
7. Dechant, Emerald V. *Improving the Teaching of Reading.* Englewood Cliffs, New Jersey: Prentice-Hall, Inc., 1964, Chaps. 10 and 11.
8. Dolch, E. W., "Am I Teaching Phonics Right?" *Elementary English,* XXXIV (April, 1957), 514–18.
9. Durr, William K. (Editor) *Reading Instruction Dimensions and Issues,* Boston: Houghton-Mifflin Co., 1967, pp. 101–125.
10. Gans, Roma. *Fact and Fiction About Phonics.* Indianapolis: Bobbs-Merrill Company, Inc., 1964.
11. Gray, William S. *On Their Own in Reading.* (Rev. Ed.) Chicago: Scott, Foresman & Company, 1960.
12. Heilman, Arthur W. *Phonics in Proper Perspective.* Columbus: Charles E. Merrill Books, Inc., 1964.
13. Love, Harold D., "An Experimental Phonics Program versus a Controlled Integral Reading Program", *Journal of Developmental Reading* (Summer, 1961), 280–82.
14. McCullough, Constance M., "Context Aids in Reading", *Reading Teacher,* XI (April, 1958), 225–29.
15. McDowell, J. B., "Report on the Phonetic Method of Teaching Children to Read", *Catholic Education, LI* (October, 1953), 506–19.
16. Smith, Henry P. and Dechant, Emerald V. *Psychology in Teaching Reading.* Englewood Cliffs, New Jersey: Prentice-Hall, Inc., 1961, Chap. 7.
17. Smith, Nila B. *Reading Instruction for Today's Children.* Englewood Cliffs, New Jersey: Prentice-Hall, Inc., 1963, Chap. 8.

6

Increasing Comprehension Skills

The end product of an effective reading program is getting pupils to grasp the meaning of the words which they perceive. Unless they understand the printed word, their reading becomes a mechanical process and is of little use to them in everyday reading experiences. Comprehension must be thought of as a "global" term, since the process is really made up of a composite of skill strands relating to such factors as reading for details, reading to get the main ideas, and differentiating between facts and opinions. These skills must be taught in a sequential manner and be evaluated through the use of standardized and informal devices.

In this chapter, the following facets related to instruction in the comprehension skill area are discussed: the meaning of comprehension; the factors which influence comprehension abilities; the development of a child's proficiency in the various comprehension skills; the comprehension skill strands; the techniques for evaluating a pupil's ability in comprehension; and materials available for developing the comprehension skills.

THE MEANING OF COMPREHENSION

As indicated in the previous section, one must not think of comprehension as consisting of a single ability. The process includes recognizing individual words, grouping the words into thought units, and relating the thought units into a meaningful sentence, paragraph, chapter, or book. For many older children and adults, this skill has not been developed to a suitable level which will allow them to grasp the total meaning of a body of related words.

Far too many people, including some teachers, equate the term, "comprehension," with reading for details. Reading for details is an important consideration, but it is only one of the facets of the comprehension act. At least eight other comprehension skill strands are described in a later portion of this chapter.

The meaning to be derived from the printed page depends in large part upon the purpose of the reader. The proficient reader has a distinct question which he seeks to answer before starting the act of reading and is not content until he finds the desired information. A student who is preparing for an examination which involves recording details from a chapter or book is wise to read slowly and grasp all important meanings; however, if he is reading to form a generalization, he should skim the material at a rapid rate.

Since a student may have widely varying levels of competency in the various skill areas, a careful evaluation of each pupil's ability in all of the comprehension skill strands should be conducted. Accordingly, one should not merely say that a given pupil is limited or strong in comprehension without explaining what particular areas he is describing.

As indicated in the following section, effective development of skills in comprehension is dependent upon a number of factors including intelligence, physical factors, word recognition ability, background of experiences, general motivation and purpose for reading, and emotional factors.

THE FACTORS WHICH INFLUENCE COMPREHENSION ABILITY

The teacher must be cognizant of the factors which are related to the formation of skill development in the total area of comprehension. The assessment of these factors helps the teacher to understand the instructional needs of each pupil. A checklist should be constructed which embodies the aspects noted in the following sections. Many of these factors can be aided by the teacher.

Intelligence

There is a positive relationship between general intelligence and ability to read for different purposes. A child's mental ability is a determining factor in calculating the number of concepts which he is able to assimilate at any given moment. The more complex comprehension skill strands demand a high level of abstract thinking. While a child with limited intelligence may remember a few details of a particular selection, he will no doubt have much difficulty in differentiating between a fact or an opinion or arriving at a generalization. In light of these conditions, an examination of each child's cumulative folder for intelligence test information should be undertaken in order to understand his demonstrated competency in the important area of comprehension.

Physical Factors

Physical factors of the type that relate to the child and to his physical surroundings have a significant effect on comprehension. A child who is excessively tired or who suffers from chronic physical illnesses such as visual or auditory defects can hardly be expected to give his complete attention to reading a selection dealing with the Kansas-Nebraska Act in which he is asked to remember significant details. Teachers must be alert to the child's physical needs and solicit the help of the school nurse or doctor when suspected physical anomalies are noted. Even though many of these conditions are outside the jurisdiction of the teacher, an understanding of the nature of these factors will help one to decide why a pupil's performance is at a certain level in the comprehension skills.

A few teachers become so engrossed in instructional procedures that they fail to take note of the physical aspects of the classroom. Rooms that are too hot, too cold, or too noisy are not appropriate settings for concentration. In order for pupils to be comfortable, attention should also be given to such matters as the size of chairs and tables employed in the classroom. Ineffective lighting caused by blinking flourescent tubes causes distraction for the child and takes his attention away from deriving maximum meaning from the printed page. These and other similar conditions should be corrected immediately.

Word Recognition Ability

The heart of the reading act is word recognition. The reader who is able to perceive words smoothly and efficiently by phonetic analysis, structural analysis, context clues, or any of the more common methods is well on his way toward grasping meaning from the printed page. Methods of teaching that overemphasize word analysis to the exclusion of word meaning may create major deficiencies in the general area of comprehension. Word calling should never take the place of reading for meaning.

A careful analysis of a child's ability in word recognition should *precede* any prescribed remedial program to correct comprehension difficulties. If the reader cannot recognize words effectively, one should concentrate on the word recognition limitations before any attempt is made to teach the child to draw a generalization or to grasp a sequence of events.

Background of Experiences

Even though a reader may be able to recognize the words in a given selection, he may have a great amount of difficulty in deriving meaning from the words due to the lack of experience with the objects or concepts which stand for the words. A child who has always lived in a large city will probably not have the same understanding for the word, "corncrib," as would a Nebraska or Iowa farm youth. By the same token, the farm child who has not visited the city can hardly have a true conception of how a subway train operates. A teacher can no doubt unlock the words found in a medical journal, but he cannot derive the same meaning from an article in the journal as a medical doctor since he probably is not familiar with the properties of many of the chemicals which might be mentioned in the selection.

The experience backgrounds of pupils can be enriched through the use of audio-visual aids such as filmstrips, films, pictures, and recordings. These tools should be used with groups of pupils to create a greater facility for grasping meaning concepts.

Motivation and Purpose for Reading

The most common cause of poor comprehension is a lack of purpose for reading. Pupils must read with the idea of answering certain guiding questions which have been formulated. The child might well use the questions which the author has posed and are commonly found at the close of the various chapters in science and social studies books. If the author has not constructed questions, then the student must be taught to form questions of his own which are suggested by the titles of the sub-topics. Still another source of questions would be those which are formulated by the various class members and the teacher.

Motivation to read is largely stimulated by the instructor's efforts in getting the pupil to read to find meaningful information. An assignment such as "read Chapter Five tomorrow" when the dismissal bell sounds without further direction does not serve to accentuate purposeful reading or to improve overall ability in comprehension. Reading for meaning can only be strengthened if readiness is built for the chapter or selection, difficult words and phrases are pronounced and defined, and guiding questions are provided for the pupils.

Emotional Factors

States of anxiety and mounting tensions can directly affect the amount of meaning and understanding which can be derived from the printed page. The child who has witnessed an argument or heated discussion between his parents at breakfast is hardly in a position to differentiate between a fact and opinion in his first hour social studies class. Many emotionally disabled pupils engage in daydreaming, while others become withdrawn or hyperactive. While one cannot hope to restructure the home condition, a study of the child's emotional symptoms can be undertaken in order to understand the level of meaning which might be expected from reading assignments. The school psychologist or guidance counselor may be in a position to offer definite suggestions with regard to pupils who are mildly disturbed.

DEVELOPING PROFICIENCY IN COMPREHENSION SKILLS

An analysis of the levels of ability in the area of comprehension varies considerably among pupils at any grade level. The scale of comprehension may range from little or no meaning to complete understanding. Not only does the degree of comprehension exist among pupils, but within pupils as well. Norman, a seventh grade student, was observed on one occasion in which he "parroted" details from a selection to his teacher. His teacher was quite dismayed to discover, however, that he was totally unable to draw a conclusion from all of the details.

The maximum development of the various skills in comprehension among all students calls for the adherence to certain guidelines by all teachers. The following statements should be remembered in designing effective programs in comprehension.

Guidelines for Teaching the Comprehension Skills

1. *Comprehension is a sum total of many skills.* Help each child develop the ability to read with many degrees of comprehension—to generalize when needed, to read for details, to secure an isolated fact, or to read to discern whether a statement is a fact or an opinion. The good reader reads for a variety of purposes and adjusts his reading speed and techniques in light of his reading purpose.

2. *If comprehension skills are to be developed adequately, instruction must be of a sequential, direct nature.* Plans for each reading lesson must indicate that instruction is aimed directly toward teaching the comprehension skill strands. While some pupils will probably develop a few of the nearly two dozen skills on their own, the entire job cannot be completed unless instruction is planned to accomplish this objective. The reading program for the formal developmental period and the different content area subjects must evidence careful planning in order that each skill is taught at a particular grade level and reinforced at later grade levels.

3. *Meaningful practice must be provided once a skill has been taught.* If lasting ability in a skill area is achieved, one must construct assignments which will lend practice regarding a skill which has been recently introduced. Little profit is to be gained from teaching a group of students how to form judgments and differentiate between facts and opinions and then constructing succeeding assignments whereby details are constantly demanded.

4. *To teach the comprehension skills, reading material at the pupil's*

instructional reading level must be used. Since word perception is the center of the reading act and precedes comprehension, one must not confront children with materials which contain a large number of difficult words which they cannot pronounce. A pupil who cannot pronounce at least 95 per cent of the running words of a given selection should not use that material in comprehension exercises. He must not be hampered by frustration level material, since his attention will be diverted to his word-attack problems and the original comprehension skill goal will be lost. Informal inventories and readability formulas should be applied to both basal reading and content area materials to insure that the teaching selections are at least at the instructional level.

5. *Periodic and continuous evaluation of a child's comprehension skill development should be a part of the total reading instruction.* Teacher-made tests, standardized instruments (such as *The Nelson Reading Test* and *The Iowa Tests of Basic Skills*), and careful observation should be used to determine each pupil's level of skill in the various comprehension areas. Good teaching practices must always be constructed to aid the individual child with his limitations and to further strengthen his areas of competency. The employment of a number of evaluative devices will help to discover the appropriate information which will in turn make possible the completion of the preceding objective. (A discussion of the use of evaluative instruments is included later in this chapter.)

6. *The questioning techniques employed by the teacher will determine to a large extent the reading purposes which will be followed by the pupils.* If children in a particular classroom are always asked such questions as "How many goats did Uncle Ben have?" "What color were the goats?" or "How large were the goats?", they will soon understand that they are always to read for facts and for no other purpose. Unfortunately, this type of questioning exists in far too many situations. Children must be taught to read for many purposes and to use a number of techniques. They must be made to understand that factual type reading is only one of many skills which should be developed.

7. *Comprehension skills must be taught by every teacher in every content area from kindergarten through the university levels.* Instruction in reading skills must never be thought of as being the sole responsibility of the English teacher, the primary teacher, or some other teacher or group of teachers. The chemistry teacher is the one who must assume the responsibility for the detailed reading of experiments. The American History teacher is the logical person to teach his pupils to arrange events in sequence and draw a conclusion from the information. Such lessons must be taught in the "natural environment" of the subject matter class.

The content area teacher cannot excuse himself from the responsibility by saying that he has not had formal training in the methods of teaching reading. If he will use the following outline, the comprehension skills of each of his pupils will be strengthened.

a. *Building a Background of Readiness.* The teacher builds a background of understanding for the material by introducing and explaining concepts and words which may be difficult or strange to the majority of the pupils. A discussion is held relative to any experiences which any of the students might have had with regard to the topic to be discussed. At this stage the learning appetites of the pupils are "whetted."

b. *Constructing Guiding Questions.* In order for the comprehension skills to be developed adequately, each student must have a purpose for reading. A list of guiding questions which have been supplied by the textbook author, the pupils, and/or the teacher should be understood thoroughly by all class members before any silent reading is assigned.

c. *Undertaking Silent Reading.* After the guiding questions have been established, each child should be asked to read the material silently (provided it is on his instructional level). During the silent reading, the teacher should notice the reading habits of the pupils to see if any undesirable habits such as finger pointing or vocalization are in evidence.

d. *Discussing the Assigned Reading.* Following the silent reading, a discussion should be conducted in light of the questions which were posed previous to the silent reading. If answers could not be found for the questions, additional source material should be suggested by the teacher.

e. *Creating Further Interest.* Additional meaning and understanding of a particular subject can be gained through the use of audio-visual aids such as pictures, films, and filmstrips. Projects involving art and drama techniques may be undertaken to stimulate further interest.

Reading authorities are not in complete agreement with respect to the exact nature of the various comprehension skill strands or when they should be introduced. This author has come to believe that there are at least nine separate skill strands which should be developed during a pupil's experience in school. Later in this chapter, these strands are listed and teaching suggestions for each of them have been provided.

Skills and Understandings Necessary for Effective Comprehension

Before discussing the various aspects of the individual strands, attention should be drawn to some concomitant training which every child should have if he is to perform satisfactorily in all areas of comprehension. The following understandings and techniques should be developed:

1. *The importance of the interpretation of punctuation should be emphasized.* These "traffic signals" have an important bearing on the meaning which should be derived from a sentence or paragraph. To stress the importance one might write several sentences with different types of punctuation to show how meaning is changed. (Examples: "The house is on fire?" "The house is on fire!") Another exercise which might be used entails the use of a paragraph or short selection in which all punctuation has been eliminated. Pupils are asked to read the selection aloud without punctuation. Later, punctuation is added and they are asked to read the selection again.

2. *Every pupil should be given practice in reading by thought units rather than by word units.* A child cannot gain skill in comprehension if he is a word-by-word reader, since he is probably giving much more attention to individual words than to what the series of words means. Good readers who have a high level of ability in comprehension exhibit the ability to group words into meaningful clusters. Practice can be given to pupils with this difficulty by providing them with selections in which spaces have been made between logical thought units. Additional practice can also be provided through the use of phrase unit flash cards.

3. *Practice should be given which will allow each student to understand and appreciate the use of such figurative language as metaphors, similes, and hyperboles.* Many modern day writers make use of figures of speech in order to clarify and amplify a particular description or explanation. In many instances the use of a figure of speech makes a point in a much better way than does the use of literal language. As an example, the expression, "the whole convention was split down the middle," may convey the extent of controversy in a group in a more descriptive way than would a matter-of-fact statement.

   Despite the usefulness of such language, many students encounter a considerable amount of difficulty in interpreting figures of speech, and unfortunately apply literal meaning when the writer intended to convey a figurative meaning. They must be taught to understand such language for what it is and appreciate the intent of the writer for employing these techniques even though such words may contain subtle, hidden meanings.

   Definite lessons should be planned such as the following to help the pupil understand figures of speech:

   a. Find a selection which contains considerable figurative language which is on the instructional level of the reader. Have him make a list of the phrases which constitute figurative language. After each phrase he should be asked to explain what each one really means.

   b. Using a similar selection, have the pupils merely underline all of the figures of speech which they find in the selection.

c. Construct a matching exercise such as the following and have the student match the figurative language segments with the intended meanings:

___(1) He was tickled to death.   a. ran quickly

___(2) Jane ran like lightning.   b. too frightened to move

___(3) The winter months have   c. was very happy
      surely flown by.   d. moved rapidly

___(4) Bob flew upstairs.   e. time seems to elapse at an un-

___(5) Mary was glued to the   usually fast rate
      stage.

4. *Help each student develop a meaningful vocabulary through the study of antonyms and synonyms, qualifying words, homonyms, and roots, prefixes, and suffixes.* In order for a high level of comprehension to take place, meaning must be attached to the various words which make up a selection. If the child lacks the proper understanding and meaning, the teacher must provide experiences which will make the phrases and words "come alive." The two methods for doing this are those activities which are of the direct-experience nature (such as a field trip) and those of the incidental experience variety such as films, filmstrips, or pictures.

Suggestions for instructional procedures relating to the development of meaningful vocabulary can be found in many language arts methods books and in the sources mentioned at the close of this chapter. Emerald Dechant's *Improving the Teaching of Reading* is especially helpful.

5. *Instruct the pupils in realizing how to read in light of the purpose and complexity of the materials.* Pupils must understand that the effective reader is one who has a reading "differential" and is able to shift to any one of several reading rate gears according to the nature of the selection. They should be taught that reading arithmetic problems requires slow, deliberate reading while reading a light, humorous novel can be accomplished at a much faster rate. At the very outset of each reading selection they must make two decisions: *the purpose they have for reading and at what rate they will read.*

Because of the present emphasis on rapid reading, some pupils have gained the mistaken idea that the good reader should read all materials at a rapid rate. A good reader has many reading rates and definite exercises and discussions such as the following will help to gain this understanding.

a. Display different kinds of reading materials such as income tax forms, newspapers, poetry, and a novel and discuss with the class the different speeds of reading which should be employed in each case.

b. Give each student a copy of factual material. Make two sets of questions—one of which requires reading for details and the other which requires reading to get a general impression. Demonstrate how one should read to answer both types of questions.

c. Distribute materials which are graded according to level of difficulty and which are written on the same topic. After directing the pupils to read the selections, call attention to the fact that the difficulty of the material affects both comprehension and rate of reading.

6. *Give pupils instruction in interpretation of topical headings and side-headings.* Authors place subheadings and sideheadings at different places in non-fiction material to aid the reader in the organization of the meaning which should be obtained from the selection. Unfortunately, many readers (including otherwise good readers) ignore these very important devices. All pupils must be taught that these aids can be a powerful tool in deriving maximum meaning from a given selection. These suggestions may help pursue this objective:

a. Provide each pupil with a copy of a textbook (such as a social studies book) which has a sizeable number of topical headings. Select a chapter which they have not previously read and ask them to look only at the headings. (Only two or three minutes should be allowed for the exercises, depending upon the length of the selection.) Ask each student to write a paragraph or two describing the basic information which the chapter contains.

b. Duplicate a three-page factual selection and leave out all subheadings and other devices. Place blanks at the places where such devices would normally be placed. Ask each student to write a suitable heading for the paragraph which follows.

7. *Provide sequential training in understanding the meaning of single words, phrases, sentences, paragraphs, chapters, and entire books in that order.* All elementary and secondary teachers must work as a unit in providing this type of training. Suggestions for the specific procedures to be followed are mentioned in the following section which is concerned with the nine basic comprehension skill strands.

THE COMPREHENSION SKILL STRANDS

As indicated earlier in this chapter, the pupil must be made to understand that the term, "comprehension," is a blanket term which is composed of at least nine segments. Pupils should be taught to read for any of the following purposes: to find the main idea; to select pertinent details; to summarize and organize; to follow directions; to predict outcomes; to differentiate between fact and opinion; to follow the writer's plan and intent; to read charts, tables, maps, and graphs; and to grasp the sequence of events.

No one of the preceding purposes is more important than any other. To be an efficient reader, necessary training must be provided for each child in all of these areas. The following sections contain a description of the meaning of each of the strands along with practical suggestions for instruction in each area.

Reading to Get the Main Idea

While many readers can remember details without difficulty, they often have trouble listing the main idea. If a reader is unable to seize the one important issue, he is hopelessly lost in a maze of details and becomes confused about the principal topic which is being discussed. This is a rather complex skill to develop since it involves a certain amount of discrimination and judgment on the part of the reader. He must be able to see the picture without any attempt to remember the distinct characteristics of each of the objects. Typically, the skill of getting the main idea is easier for gifted children than those with average or below average ability.

Skill in determining the main idea from a selection is basic to several of the other comprehension skill strands such as reading to generalize or to differentiate between fact and opinion. Skill in reading to get the main idea should be developed through the use of formal and incidental means. Several of these techniques are discussed in the following section.

1. Ask pupils to read a selection of three or four paragraphs and select from several titles which one would be most suitable. After completing the exercise discuss the reasons why certain titles would not be satisfactory.

2. List the title of a chapter along with the various sub-titles and ask each child to summarize in two or three sentences what he thinks the author has discussed.

3. Provide each student with a copy of a three paragraph nonfiction selection. List four sentences below the selection, one of which represents the main idea. Ask him to choose the main idea and to tell why the other sentences are not appropriate.

4. Give the children a copy of a newspaper or magazine which is written on their instructional level. Select an article and have them construct a sentence which represents the main idea of the writer.

5. Another variation of No. 4 is to delete the title given the story or article by the editor and ask the pupils to write an appropriate title of their choosing.

6. Make students aware of the importance of topic sentences which often state the most important idea in a paragraph or story. Indicate to them that this is usually the first sentence; however, in some instances it may be the last sentence.

7. Call attention to the introductory and concluding paragraphs of a selection. Indicate to the pupils that many times the major idea can often be found in one of these paragraphs.

Reading to get the main idea demands a rather rapid rate of reading with particular notice given to the key thought. The reader must always have a purpose or a specific question in mind before the reading is started in order that a high level of motivation may be formed.

Reading to Select Pertinent Details

Reading for details is an essential segment of reading for meaning. There are many content areas such as science and social studies which require very careful deliberate reading in order to learn how an experiment is performed or what the exact provisions of a treaty were. In mathematics one must read for details, particularly phases of the problem which are concerned with numbers and important words which are cues as to whether the reader should add, multiply, subtract, or divide.

As mentioned earlier, reading for a large number of details is a slow, methodical process which demands close attention on the part of the reader. Depending upon the powers of concentration which the reader possesses, it may be necessary to reread certain essential details in order that proper relationships may be developed. To learn isolated details and not see the relationships among these details is a fault displayed by many students at the high school and university levels.

Proficiency in reading for details can be aided if help is given to all pupils in establishing the proper purposes for reading. Silent reading should be supervised at all times and exercises checked. Students should be shown why a given answer or a set of answers is incorrect.

In some instances, when the answer to one specific question is sought, the reader must develop the facility to skim rapidly. There are many occasions when the pupil will want to find a date, a name, or a telephone number in a limited time. In a functional sense, he will be confronted with questions such as the following in arithmetic, history, and science:

1. Which number are you supposed to subtract?
2. How many sections did Mr. Smith own?
3. What are the names of the tribes which belonged to the Plains Indians?
4. What three chemicals should be mixed together in the beaker for today's experiment?
5. Who was President of the United States when the Louisiana Territory was purchased?
6. What is the principal cash crop of Honduras?
7. Which state has greater population—New York or Texas?

Reading for details is essential in all of the subject matter areas. Pupils can be helped to develop this important ability by providing exercises such as the following:

1. Have the pupils read a short factual selection silently which is about three paragraphs in length. Ask each of them to turn over the sheet and to record as many different facts from the selection as possible. The class should be told of the plan before silent reading is undertaken.

2. Using the same type of exercise as described in No. 1, ask the students to underline all phrases which are keys to important details. An exercise such as the following is useful for this purpose.

— —

Directions: Underline all words and phrases which are keys to important details. The first sentence is done for you.

The <u>first President</u> of the <u>United States</u> was <u>George Washington</u>. He was <u>born</u> in <u>1732</u> and was <u>destined</u> to be a <u>surveyor</u> and a <u>military leader</u>. He was a tall man and came from a wealthy family. He died in 1799.

3. List the main points of an article and ask each child to record all of the details which are related to each of the main points.

4. After the pupils have read a section of material which contains a large number of details, provide them with additional copies of the same material in which blanks have been left on which they are to record significant details such as names, places, and dates. Give them the original copy and let them check their papers in order that they might understand the types of details which need more training emphasis.

5. Let the pupils look at a picture which contains a large number of objects. Ask them to describe the picture using as many factual words and phrases as possible.

6. The "Gold Mine" game is enjoyed by all children. The teacher reads a ten-sentence set of directions describing the procedures which must be followed in order to find a mythical gold mine which is located in the school building. Any child who can repeat the directions, in order, can lay "claim" to the treasure.

7. After having read a selection such as one dealing with the growth in population in the United States from 1900 to the present, ask each pupil to prepare a chart or bar graph which would illustrate this information.

8. Asking pupils to write a news report stressing the concepts "who," "what," "when," "why," and "where" is a good way to impress upon them the need for remembering details.

One should constantly remind pupils that many details are contained in a given selection and that they must decide which details are significant for the purpose they have in mind. Facts and figures are significant when they relate to a main idea.

Reading to Summarize and Organize

One of the more intricate skills in comprehension is the ability to gather together all of the details and subsequent main ideas and compile a summary of the information. To be able to make the summary, the reader must be able to see the relationship between the details and the main ideas and how to make these clear to another person who is reading the summary. One must not feel that it is always necessary to write the summaries. An efficient reader naturally organizes materials in his mind at the conclusion of a reading session. If the material is to be put to active use at some later date, it should be written to preserve the essential facts and main ideas. These summaries would be especially helpful in such subjects as social science and literature, while they would be less useful in subjects such as mathematics and science where quantities of exact information must be memorized.

Exercises such as the following may be used to promote proficiency in the summarizing skills:

1. Have students read a poem or short non-fiction selection and ask them to select the statement which best represents a summation of the information presented.

2. Indicate to pupils the importance of such words as *first, second, initially,* and *finally.* These words give a hint to important statements and thus aid in the formation of a summary. Attention should be given to the words whether they are used in print or are spoken.

3. Organization of a topic can be achieved through outlining. Proper instruction should be given to the pupils in the use of Roman numerals for major headings, capital letters for major sub-headings, and numbers for minor sub-headings. Such a procedure would be especially useful with regard to such a topic as "Three Steps to Reading Success."

4. Provide copies of a summary and the selection from which the summaries were made. Make a deliberate effort to include statements in the summary which are not pertinent. Ask the pupils to draw a line through the irrelevant sentences.

5. An interesting alternative to No. 3 is to use an overhead projector and show an outline of a topic on the screen. Purposely place different aspects of the topic in an incorrect order and ask the pupils to tell why the outline is incorrect.

6. Provide each student with a news article and ask him to supply a suitable headline. Compare the headlines supplied by the pupils with the original headline which was supplied by the newspaper editor.

7. The organization of a book or bulletin can be studied through an analysis of the table of contents page. A related activity is to place strips of paper over the title of a chapter and the various sub-topics and ask pupils to supply this information after reading the chapter or section.

8. Ask each pupil to read a fable and to select the most logical moral from a list of possible morals which are listed at the conclusion of the story.

The ability to summarize and organize is one of the most important skills to be developed, especially for the pupil at the intermediate and upper grade levels.

Reading to Follow Directions

During an average lifetime, a given individual is required to demonstrate his ability to follow printed directions. A large number of adults have not developed this skill; therefore, many valuable hours are wasted during a given year. Various individuals have need for completing income tax forms, studying recipe books, reading directions in a manual, and reading the "fine print" in a contract.

In order to prepare our citizens for these tasks, each pupil must be provided with systematic training in this very important skill. As a basis for the training, the children must be taught to listen carefully in order to construct a mental picture of what is to be remembered. Practice in learning to follow directions must make use of the materials and subjects which are a part of everyday assignments in the content areas. For instance, directions might be given to the pupils relative to the construction of plaster Christmas balls as part of a seasonal art project. Each child should gain the feeling that to learn to follow directions enables him to participate more fully in class activities.

One must insist that each pupil read the directions for an assignment himself if he is to feel a complete responsibility for interpreting written directions correctly. The teacher's attitude with respect to the skill is important. If she is satisfied with "nearly" correct responses or condones "careless" attitudes, the pupils can hardly be expected to develop efficiency in this area. They must understand that the directions for completing a standardized test or a workbook page must be done accurately if they are to receive full credit for their efforts.

Practice materials used for developing this skill *must* be on the instructional reading levels of the pupils. A reader cannot follow directions if he is unable to recognize certain key words. Children should be asked to circle or underline the occasional word which they cannot pronounce. Appropriate help should be given at a later time with respect to the difficult words.

Some activities for teaching pupils to follow directions are the following:

1. With primary children, many directions should be written on the chalkboard such as "Put your books in your desk," "Pick up all of the crayons," or "It is time for recess."

2. Ask various pupils to read announcements to their fellow classmates and observe which pupils are able to follow the directions contained in the announcements.

3. A number of individual directions should be printed on one large sheet. Each pupil is to find the direction relating to him and perform the duty requested.

4. Except for a brief introduction of the purpose for a given exercise, pupils should always be expected to read and follow the directions. If the directions state that a "T" should be placed before all true statements and a child places a plus sign instead, all of these statements should be scored as being incorrect. Initially the pupil may feel this is a harsh practice; however, an impression will be made regarding the importance of following directions precisely.

5. The directions for a given activity may be printed in a "scrambled" sequence. Each student should be asked to place the statements in proper order.

6. Learning to follow directions accurately can be emphasized through the use of game activities such as the following:
   Read all of the following directions accurately before completing any exercise.
   a. Write the third letter of your last name in the following space ___.
   b. Stand and say your first and last name.
   (Continue similar directions until at least twenty items have been compiled. For the last item write: "Make no marks on this side of the page. Write your name on the back and give the sheet to your teacher.")

7. Brief directions can be given orally for performing an experiment or making a project. Pupils should be asked to write the directions from memory. Papers should be exchanged and various students should be asked if they can follow the directions which are written.

Reading to Predict Outcomes

The mature reader is one who can assimilate a few important details, think ahead, and guess the outcome of a particular selection. In order to predict the outcome in an accurate manner, the reader must be able to read for details, have a rich background of experience, and be able to exhibit a reasonable attention span.

Pupils can learn to become "active" readers by developing this skill. A variety of guiding questions can be used—sometimes they should be given at the outset of the selection to encourage students to guess what is going to happen, while at other times it is more constructive to have them read several paragraphs of a selection and then predict how the story is concluded.

Some of the following suggestions may be used for developing this skill:

1. Provide pupils with the first three paragraphs of a story. The third paragraph should build to a climax. Ask them to complete the story in three more paragraphs.

2. Ask students to predict what will happen when three different chemicals are mixed in a test tube. (It is assumed that the properties of these chemicals have been studied previously.)

3. Multiple-choice statements can be constructed which will develop the skill of predicting outcomes. As an example, one might write: "If black paint and white paint are mixed, the resulting color will be: (1) green; (2) gray; (3) blue; (4) yellow."

4. The skill can be practiced profitably in arithmetic by asking pupils to estimate answers to certain problems. If they are able to estimate accurately, they can ascertain the correctness of a given answer with a greater degree of accuracy.

Reading to Differentiate Between Fact and Opinion

Of all the skills which have been enumerated to this point, the skill of critical reading may well be one of the most important neglected areas in language arts instruction. All forms of communication bombard both children and adults to take sides in an issue or to buy a particular product.

In a democratic society, it is imperative that every citizen weigh carefully every statement read or heard. Propaganda techniques such as name calling, testimonials, glittering generalizations, the band wagon effect, and identification with well-known persons are to be found in editorials, news stories, subject matter books, and advertisements. The attitudes of many supposedly sophisticated adult readers with regard to critical reading concepts are at a surprisingly underdeveloped level. The tendency among many readers to accept printed statements as being true is widespread. The adult or child who believes everything that he notes in print is an easy target for an unscrupulous salesman or devious propagandist. He is in a constant state of confusion, especially during a period when different sides of an issue are printed in a newspaper with appropriate "statistics."

Instruction in differentiating between facts and opinions must begin in the primary grades if the skill is to be developed adequately. Small children should be asked and indeed encouraged to express opinions regarding the truthfulness of given statements which they find in various selections. They should be taught the difference between reality and fantasy and be able to recognize each in its proper context.

In order to be a good critical reader, a child must read in a questioning manner in order to forestall any incorrect impression which might be brought about by the writer's prejudices or biases. He thinks with the writer and attempts to answer the questions which are included in a later paragraph in this section.

Reading critically is a relatively slow, phrase by phrase, sentence by sentence operation and requires the careful attention and concentration of the reader. He is alert to the several propaganda techniques and deals with them accordingly.

Pupils can be aided materially in learning to read critically. A mere knowledge of the importance of critical reading is not enough to insure that they know how to apply the skill. The children need direct training as suggested by the following exercises:

1. Every child should be taught to read printed material with the following questions in mind:

    a. Who wrote the material and what are his qualifications?

    b. When was the material written?

    c. How does the information supplied by this author compare with the information supplied on this subject by other writers?

    d. Are there any propaganda devices such as "name calling" or "card stacking" which can be noted?

    e. Is the material written for a particular class of readers?

    f. What is the writer's chief purpose for compiling the material?

    g. Where was the selection written and under what circumstances?

    h. Are there inferences indicated which are unsavory?

    i. Does the writer support his point of view with appropriate evidence?

2. Give each pupil a sheet on which the following statements have been printed. Discuss each statement with them in light of the questions indicated in No. 1.

    a. Mr. George Brown, a farmer, said that all commercial planes should not travel faster than 300 miles per hour.

    b. A candidate for Congress recently indicated that unemployment in the United States was at an all time high.

    c. The best news is broadcast on radio station BLAB.

    d. A recent survey indicated that FIZ was the most popular of all soft drinks now on the market.

    e. Buy a Timeright watch—it's later than you think.

    f. The leading cause of automobile wrecks in the United States is excessive speed.

    g. Brazil has a higher population than France according to Knowitall encyclopedia.

    h. A number of leading citizens from X country have been convicted for committing serious crimes in this country. Americans would do well to avoid visiting X country in the future.

    i. The most beautiful place in Kansas is the Medicine Lodge Peace Treaty Grounds.

    j. The author of our social studies book says that the state of Vermont has more lakes which are suitable for fishing than any other state.

    k. Vernon, one of our pupils, said that a man on TV mentioned that Lonzo Delano Montgomery would be the next mayor of our city.

3. Help students determine whether an author is qualified to write about a certain topic. An exercise similar to the following may be prepared:

For each of the following names of books and articles, underline the name of the author which you feel should be the most qualified to write on the suggested subject.

    a. *The Missile Gap and How to Close It*
       J. Arthur Browne, Professor of English, State University
       General Leland H. Trunwick, United States Air Force
       J. R. Smithizer, Clerk, A-R Department Store

    b. "How to Be a More Efficient Reader"
       Mr. C. E. Dobbingten, Manager, Noleak Tire Supply
       Mr. Wright Cluberton, Mayor, Springton Village
       Mrs. Ruth Madersting, Professor of Elementary Education, Nearby University

4. Construct three or four paragraphs relating to a given subject. Purposely place several irrelevant statements in the selection. Ask the pupils to draw a line through all such statements.

5. As a part of a social studies activity, ask the children to select the most appropriate source for finding information relative to the latest population of the country being studied. Place the following books on the resource table: the latest copy of the *World Almanac;* a volume from a 1959 set of a popular encyclopedia; and a textbook with a 1962 copyright. Ask them to select the proper source.

6. After studying different propaganda techniques such as the use of testimonials, use advertisements to analyze the techniques employed.

7. Have pupils underline words and phrases in a selection which are employed by the writer to evoke anger or emotion.

8. Encourage students to bring statements from a newspaper or book which indicate opposite viewpoints on a given subject.

Differentiating between a fact and an opinion (or critical reading as it is discussed here) is one of the higher comprehension skills. Knowing when and how to apply the skill is a characteristic of the effective reader.

One should remember that some types of reading must be dealt with in a literal sense and cannot be read critically. Completing an income tax form or following the directions in a "do-it-yourself" manual must be completed as specified. The teacher's job is to train the pupils to know when to apply literal or critical reading skills.

Reading to Follow the Writer's Plan and Intent

A good writer develops an order or sequence for the types of information which he intends to present in a given body of material. He properly determines the importance of each item and places the topics in the proper setting for logical assimilation by the reader. Reading material which is designed to inform usually contains a brief introduction, a body, and a summary of the total information. Other types of materials may be of the fictional variety while still others may be written in such a manner as to persuade the reader to take a position on an issue. An efficient reader must determine if the material is factual, informational, fictional, or satirical in nature.

Pupils need to be alerted with respect to the organizational procedures employed by the writer such as his use of headings, subheadings, marginal notes, summaries, and questions. Most writers are consistent in their use of these devices. An understanding of these aspects helps the reader to achieve greater overall comprehension of the topics and to read with greater ease.

Reading to follow the writer's plan and intent is one of the important skill strands to be stressed particularly at the middle grade, upper grade, and adult reading levels. Some suggestions for teaching pupils in this skill area are as follows:

1. Ask pupils to outline materials in light of the writer's organizational procedures.

2. Demonstrate the plan of attack used for the first and last chapters of a given book in order to demonstrate the consistency of the author in presenting the body of material.

3. Ask various students to present different kinds of informational-type books and to comment on the different organizational approaches used by the writers.

4. Give each pupil a two or three page bulletin. Ask them to determine if the body of material is informational, fictional, factual, or satirical in nature. An appropriate discussion should be included.

Reading to Understand Charts, Tables, Maps, and Graphs

In the areas of social studies and science, authors find that the use of a map, a graph, a table, or a chart is the most appropriate way to convey certain graphic information to the reader. Teaching pupils how to interpret these aids is very important, since in most instances the elementary teacher instructs in all subjects.

From the first grade upward, pupils are expected to make use of these aids in the proper context. In all too many instances children have not been taught the value of these tools. Some pupils have the habit of skipping past this kind of material without realizing the relationship of the aid and the accompanying explanation.

When a table or graph is first introduced in a book, it is necessary to instruct the pupils on how to interpret it. A study of the special terms which accompany a map or chart must be undertaken in order that each student will understand the meaning of such terms as "latitude," "longitude," and "average."

Attention should be directed to the value of pictures and how information may be derived from studying and "reading" such pictures. The association between the charts and graphs and pictures must be made clear.

Instruction in this important area should be of both the incidental and planned varieties. A careful evaluation should be made early in the school year of each pupil's aptitude in this area and consequent plans made for corrective teaching in order to remove limitations. The incidental use of any or all of the following suggestions should be of value:

1. After calling attention to a graph or chart, ask the students to respond to such questions as "What is the average temperature for the month of January in Miami, Florida?" or "What country has the highest population?"

2. Supply the pupils with a body of statistics and ask them to make a graph or chart which will include this information. Constructive criticism of each child's project should follow. (The information used for this project should be meaningful. The number of pupils enrolled in each grade in each school might well be an example.)

3. Ask the class members to make a map of the school neighborhood. Teach the importance and use of colors to denote population density and/or altitude. Check each map to see that each child understands the use of proportion with respect to distances among objects.

4. With the use of a map, require each pupil to find an example of each of the following: *fiord, river, sea, capitol, valley, mountain,* and *ocean.*

5. Multiple-choice type exercises can be employed to evaluate a child's understanding of a chart, map, or graph. After showing a contour

map of the United States, one might construct an exercise such as the following:

a. The highest mountain in the United States is
___ Mt. McKinley
___ Mt. Everest
___ Mt. Mailton
___ Pikes Peak

b. St. Louis is situated by which of the following rivers?
___ Missouri
___ Mississippi
___ Arkansas
___ Red

c. Which of the following states has the highest average elevation?
___ Kansas
___ Vermont
___ Colorado
___ Florida

d. Of which state is Lincoln the Capitol?
___ North Dakota
___ Montana
___ Maine
___ Nebraska

6. Encourage pupils to give explanatory talks concerning vacation trips which they have taken. Maps should be used by the speaker. Ask the various speakers to explain if the map represents the topography of the area correctly.

Reading to Grasp the Sequence of Events

In the area of social studies, the ability to understand historical material is contingent upon being able to follow a sequence of events. For many pupils, events tend to run together and little understanding of the total chain of events can be achieved.

The reader must be able to catalogue events in order to understand the *who, what, when,* and *where* of given situations. The use of time lines and charts to plot the sequence of events may be a meaningful manner for showing the importance of this skill. By making use of time lines, for example, the entire sequence of events can be continuously charted as the school year progresses. Additional suggestions such as the following may also be employed:

1. After reading a story to the class members, ask them to make a chart showing what happened first, second, etc.

2. As indicated earlier, time lines can be constructed which would employ pictures as well as line facts. The line can be planned for a period of one week, six weeks, a semester, or even a school year.

3. Many incidental questions can be asked which will stimulate proficiency in this area. While studying the different aspects of the Civil War, one might ask, "Was Nebraska a state at that time?" or "Was Theodore Roosevelt president after or before this event?"

4. Present different segments of a story in scrambled form, and ask the class members to rearrange the parts in proper sequence.

TECHNIQUES FOR EVALUATING A PUPIL'S ABILITY IN COMPREHENSION

The evaluation procedures involved in evaluating ability in the comprehension skills should make use of standardized tests, informal reading tests such as a subjective reading inventory, and the careful observations of the teacher.

A number of group standardized reading tests are available to the teacher in the area of comprehension. A representative sampling of these tests is given here:

California Reading Test. Grades 1, 2, 3, lower 4, 4–6, 7–9, 9–14. Four forms. Time: 20–25 minutes. California Test Bureau.

Chapman-Cook Speed of Reading Test. Grades 4–8. Two forms. Time: 2½ minutes. Educational Test Bureau.

Chicago Reading Tests. Grades 1–2, 2–4, 4–6, 6–8. Three forms. Time: 31–45 minutes. E. M. Hale and Company.

Developmental Reading Tests: Primary Reading. Grades 1–3 (three levels: primer reading, lower primary reading, upper primary reading). One form. Time: 10–15 minutes for each part. Lyons & Carnahan.

Diagnostic Reading Tests. Grades K–4, 4–6, 7–13. Two to eight forms. Time: 15–60 minutes depending upon the section. Committee on Diagnostic Testing, Inc.

Gates-MacGinitie Reading Tests. Grades 1, 2, 3, 4–6, 7–9, 10–12. Time: Seven to fifty minutes depending upon the section. Teachers College Press.

Metropolitan Achievement Tests: Reading. Grades 1, 2, 3, 3–4, 5, 6, 7, 8. Three forms. Time: about 45 minutes. Harcourt, Brace, and World.

Nelson Silent Reading Test. Grades 3–9. Two forms. Time: 30 minutes. Houghton-Mifflin Company.

Sangren-Woody Reading Test. Grades 4–8. Two forms. Time: 27 minutes. Harcourt, Brace, and World.

SRA Reading Record. Grades 7–12. One form. Time: 40 minutes. Science Research Associates.

Tests of Study Skills. Grades 4–9. Two forms. Time: 60 minutes. Steck-Vaughn Company.

Work Study Skills: Iowa Every-Pupil Tests of Basic Skills. Grades 3–5, 5–9. Four forms. Time: 47–77 minutes. Houghton-Mifflin Company.

In addition to standardized tests, use should also be made of such informal devices as the subjective reading inventory which is described in

Chapter 1. Careful observation of each child's everyday performance in each of the comprehension skill areas should be a part of the total evaluation.

MATERIALS AVAILABLE FOR DEVELOPING COMPREHENSION SKILLS

A large number of commercial materials are presently available for use as teaching aids in developing skill in comprehension. The following is a representative sampling of commercial aids. Since prices of materials are subject to change, no attempt is made to list them. Addresses of publishers can be found in the appendix sections.

Publisher	Title	Reading Level	Interest Level
Barnell, Loft, Ltd.	*Specific Skills Series*		
	Using the Context, Books A–F (Six Booklets in Series)	1–6	1–12
	Getting The Facts, Books A–D (Four Booklets in Series)	1–4	1–12
	Locating The Answer, Books A–D (Four Booklets in Series)	1–4	1–12
	Following Directions, Books A–D (Four Booklets in Series)	1–4	1–12
	Drawing Conclusions	1	1–12
	Getting The Main Idea	1	1–12
Bureau of Publications, Teachers College	*McCall-Crabbs Standard Test Lessons in Reading,* Books A–D (Five in Series)	3–12	3–12
	Gates-Peardon Reading Exercises		
	Introductory Level A and B	2	2–12
	Preparatory Level A and B	3	3–12
	Elementary SA, RD, FD	4	4–12
	(Ten Booklets in Series)	5	4–12
Educational Developmental Laboratories	*Comprehension Power: Paragraphs and Sentences* (Four Booklets and Film-strips in Series)	3–6	
	EDL Study Skills Library (Boxes related to Science, Social Studies, and Reference. Each box has materials from the third through ninth grade reading levels.)	3–9	3–10
J. B. Lippincott	*Reading for Meaning* Books 4–12 (Nine booklets in Series)	4–12	4–12

Macmillan Company	*The Macmillan Reading Spectrum* Comprehension, Levels 1–6 (Six booklets in Series)	3–8	4–12
McCormick-Mathers	*Building Reading Skills* (Six booklets in Series)	1–6	1–9
McGraw-Hill	*Conquests in Reading*	4	4–8
	Webster Classroom Reading Clinic	1–3	4–9
Charles E. Merrill	*Reading Skilltexts* (Eight consumable texts in Series.)	1–12	1–12
	Building Reading Power	5–up	5–12
	Reading Skilltapes	1–12	1–12
Random House	*Skilpacers* Finding The Main Idea Recall of Factual Detail Following Sequence of Events Locating Answers Predicting Outcomes Cause and Effect Reference Skills Summarizing Skimming and Learning Grouping and Categorizing Picture Interpretation Context Clues Understanding Character	5–6	5–12
Reader's Digest Services	*Reading Skill Builder*, Book 1 Parts 1–2	1–2	1–6
	Reading Skill Builder, Book 2 Parts 1–2–3	2	2–12
	Reading Skill Builder, Book 3 Parts 1–2–3	3	3–12
	Reading Skill Builder, Book 4 Parts 1–2–3	4	4–12
	Reading Skill Builder, Book 5 Parts 1–2–3	5	5–12
	Reading Skill Builder, Book 6 Parts 1–2–3	6	6–12
	Advanced Reading Skill Builder Books 1–2–3–4	7–8	7–12
Science Research Associates	*Reading Laboratory* IIa, IIb, IIc	2–9	4–12
	Reading Laboratory IIIa	3–11	7–12
	Reading Laboratory IVa	8–14	8–14

Pilot Library Series:

	Pilot Library IIa	2–7	2–9
	Pilot Library IIc	4–9	4–11
	Pilot Library IIIb	5–12	5–14
Reading for Understanding:			
	General Edition	5–16	5–16
	Junior Edition	3–8	3–10
	Senior Edition	8–12	8–14
Steck-Vaughn	Reading Essentials Series	1–8	1–10

There are at least eighty or more publishers who produce commercial reading materials for teachers; the preceding list constitutes a mere sampling of the more commonly used materials. The fact that a material is listed does not necessarily mean this author endorses that material.

The selection of material should be done with utmost care to avoid duplication and unnecessary drill. No aid is so *complete* that other materials are not essential. Use any printed material or mechanical aid with children in the same manner as a physician dispenses drugs for his patients. Become familiar with each child's instructional needs and then purchase or construct materials which will satisfy those needs.

Summary

One must not think of comprehension as being a single ability. The process is a global concept and demands competency on the part of the reader in several definable areas. The reader's level of intelligence, physical factors, word recognition ability, background of experiences, motivation, and emotional stability are salient factors with respect to the level of comprehension which he might reach.

A number of important guidelines have been described in this chapter which should be remembered when instructing in the comprehension skills. These admonitions should be kept in mind regardless of the skill being stressed at a given time.

Sequential instruction must be given in at least nine comprehension skill strands: reading to get the main idea; reading to select pertinent details; reading to summarize and organize; reading to follow directions; reading to predict outcomes; reading to differentiate between fact and opinion (critical reading); reading to follow the writer's plan and intent; reading to understand charts, tables, maps, and graphs; and reading to grasp the sequence of events.

The evaluation of comprehension skills must be continuous and periodic and involve the use of informal and standardized measures. Before using standardized tools, careful study should be made to see if the purposes of the instruments evaluate the instructional goals which are being pursued.

There are many commercial materials which are available for instruction in the area of comprehension. No one aid is so well constructed that it can meet the needs of all pupils in the classroom. Materials must be selected carefully.

Selected References

1. Barbe, Walter B. *Educator's Guide to Personalized Reading Instruction.* Englewood Cliffs, New Jersey: Prentice-Hall, Inc., 1961. Chaps. 7 and 8.
2. Bond, Guy L. and Tinker, Miles A. *Reading Difficulties: Their Diagnosis and Correction.* New York: Appleton-Century-Crofts, 1967. Chap. II.
3. Carter, Homer L. J. and McGinnis, Dorothy J. *Teaching Individuals to Read.* Boston: D. C. Heath and Company, 1962. Chap. 6.
4. Dechant, Emerald. *Improving the Teaching of Reading.* Englewood Cliffs, New Jersey: Prentice-Hall, Inc., 1964. Chap. 13.
5. Gans, Roma. *Common Sense in Teaching Reading.* Indianapolis: The Bobbs-Merrill Company, Inc., 1963. Chaps. 10 and 11.
6. Harris, Albert. *Effective Teaching of Reading.* New York: David McKay Company, Inc., 1962. Chap. 11.
7. King, Martha L., Bernice D. Ellinger, and Willavene Wolf (Editors). *Critical Reading.* New York: J. B. Lippincott Company, 1967. Entire volume.
8. McKim, Margaret and Caskey, Helen. *Guiding Growth in Reading.* New York: The Macmillan Company, 1963. Chap. 12.
9. Russell, David. *Children Learn to Read.* Waltham, Massachusetts: Blaisdell Publishing Company, 1961. Chap. 14.
10. Smith, Henry P. and Dechant, Emerald. *Psychology in Teaching Reading.* Englewood Cliffs, New Jersey: Prentice-Hall, Inc., 1961. Chap. 8.
11. Smith, Nila B. *Reading Instruction for Today's Children.* Englewood Cliffs, New Jersey: Prentice-Hall, Inc., 1963. Chap. 9.
12. Witty, Paul A., Freeland, Alma Moore, and Grotberg, Edith B. *The Teaching of Reading.* Boston: D. C. Heath and Company, 1966. Chap. 10.

7

Reading Skills in the Content Areas

Most teachers at the elementary levels are seriously concerned regarding the procedures for building developmental reading skills during the school period generally designated for such purposes. Pupils are typically grouped according to reading abilities and appropriate materials are used. The reading selections typically consist of narrative-type stories which most pupils find enjoyable when the content is on their respective instructional levels. Many of these same pupils, however, encounter a considerable amount of difficulty when mastering the various texts and source books in the areas of science, mathematics, and social studies. If children are to read content materials successfully, provision must be made for specific instruction to insure this objective. While there is a general body of reading skills which applies to the total content field, the skills in each area have unique differences which should be explained.

To provide practical helps in meeting teacher responsibilities in this important instructional area, a discussion of the following topics is included in this chapter: difficulties involved in reading content area materials; the study skills involved in content area reading; reading in the social studies; reading in mathematics; reading in science; evaluation of content area reading skills; and a summary of the total discussion.

DIFFICULTIES INVOLVED IN READING CONTENT AREA MATERIALS

There are a number of inherent differences in the reading tasks involved in reading narrative-type stories and the selections found in content area textbooks and sourcebooks. In this section, brief explanations of these difficulties are presented in order to develop a clearer understanding of the necessity for providing sequential instruction in content reading skills.

Precise suggestions for helping pupils with these difficulties are included in later sections of this chapter.

Coping with the Compact Presentation of Content Materials

Textbooks in the science and mathematics areas are typically written in a very compact manner with a large number of significant facts and figures presented in a small amount of space. While a child may find it possible to read at a rapid rate to find a main idea in a light, humorous story in his basal reader, he finds it imperative to consider each and every word in the arithmetic problem if he is to arrive at the correct answer. An inaccurate reading of a science experiment may well result in a minor explosion in the science laboratory. At the adult level, one may enjoy novels and be able to read them at a rapid rate; however, an income tax audit may result if significant directions have not been followed in completing an income tax return. Teachers have the responsibility for showing pupils how to shift rate of reading according to compactness of the reading matter and the purposes which they have in mind.

Understanding the Amount of New Words Introduced

The vocabulary found in many of the content areas, especially social studies, is introduced more rapidly than in narrative material and is complex in many instances. Technical terms such as "vassal" and "hieroglyphic" are presented together with long multisyllabic words such as "totalitarian" and "miscalculation." Abstract terms such as "credibility" and "liberty" are used in various contexts with little or no further explanation. The pupil's understanding of the words is dependent upon his background of experience (even though it might be limited), his ability to recognize and pronounce the words, and his proficiency in using context clues. Vocabulary which is new to the pupils must be explained according to the dictionary definitions and then proper applications made of the words in succeeding oral discussions and written assignments. Quite frequently, the reader finds that the definition for a word in one subject is quite different from the meaning in another subject. Each child should have access to a dictionary which will lend him the needed help in trying to discover which of several definitions may be applicable to the material being read. In selecting books for pupils, one should be alert to the amount and kinds of new vocabulary introduced so that the less able children will not become discouraged in using such materials.

Comprehending the Myriad of Concepts Presented

A concept is much more than a single word, sentence, or paragraph. It is developed as an abstraction after the child has demonstrated his ability to pronounce and understand one or more words. In many instances the pupil is confronted with paragraphs such as the following:

> The maze of social circumstances which precipitated the altercation were of a variety unheard of in the upper socioeconomic strata of society. To cope with the complex conditions, the social forces of the community took things in their own hands and attempted to bring order out of chaos.

In the paragraph just presented, one immediately notes lengthy sentences which are complex in structure. Several words and phrases in the selection may be strange to the student: "maze," "precipitated," "altercation," "strata," "social forces," and "chaos." The teacher's job is not only to teach the content of the lesson, but also to point out how to master the content. The concepts in each content area must be presented in the language of the subject, and pupils must grasp them and make them a part of their total experience.

Reading in a Variety of Sources

Because no one textbook contains all of the possible information which should be studied in any one particular field, wide reading is demanded in a variety of sources. Each teacher has the distinct responsibility for guiding students into wide reading in supplementary texts of varying difficulty. This aspect will present some difficulties for the pupils, since certain of the social studies areas may be written in many different ways according to the dictates of the authors. As an example, authors of geography texts have a writing style quite divergent from that employed by history text authors. In each case the students must become acquainted with the author and understand his style of writing.

As indicated previously, supplementary books must be provided which are written on a number of reading levels, since students in a given grade may represent as many as four to eight reading grade levels. Each student should be able to find a book which suits his reading and interest level. The librarian and school principal can be of much help in selecting books from many different levels of difficulty.

Facing a Mass of Unrelated Facts

An elementary or upper grade student is often faced with content area materials which contain a large number of seemingly unrelated facts in a small section of a chapter. If he is to understand the significance of the topic under consideration, he must be able to retain and organize these facts and place them in some meaningful learning pattern. If a large number of dates and places are included in a brief discussion of "Wars In This Century," the pupil must have mastered the skills of organization described in the previous chapter dealing with comprehension.

Understanding Relationships Among the Content Area Subjects

Pupils need to understand that they cannot read content area texts and divorce each set of factual presentations. Mathematics and science are inextricably related as are history, geography, and government. All of the information among these various major subject areas has really been woven into one meaningful unit. One must never presume that these relationships are obvious to the reader. The elementary teacher needs to demonstrate to the children that the chapter concerning farming in the Great Plains which was read in the geography text during the morning social studies period has some correlation and serves as a background for understanding the nature and kinds of soil being studied during the science period in the afternoon.

Reading Content Area Materials Critically

Many of the selections found in narrative-type material are read by pupils for genuine pleasure without a thought of being confronted with serious critical reading problems. As indicated in the previous chapter, many books which one may use for studying social studies topics and various social issues may contain statements which reflect mere opinions rather than proven facts. Content area materials force the reader to judge the pertinence and authenticity of remarks found in the written matter. Unless the pupils have been given very specific training in critical reading skills, they will have difficulty in recognizing conflicting statements which appear in the text and related materials.

THE STUDY SKILLS INVOLVED IN CONTENT AREA READING

Difficulties in reading content area materials can be partially overcome if the reader is equipped with certain study skills which are described and explained in this section. While these skills are emphasized in varying degrees in the different basal supplementary reading materials, the teacher must assume the responsibility for introducing, demonstrating, and reinforcing these skills with content materials.

SURVEYING OR PREVIEWING THE MATERIAL

In every major military conflict, each country involved in the war makes every attempt to gain knowledge concerning the enemy's source of supplies; the location of his armies, factories, and transportation routes; and as much information as possible concerning his battle strategy. Field commanders find that victories are more easily won when information of this type is available. The successful reader "attacks" reading material in the content areas with the same degree of vigor.

The child should learn to take immediate notice of the title of the chapter or chapters, headings and subheadings, graphic and illustrative material, the topic sentences, and the introductory and summary statements. While using this technique to gain a general impression of the subject matter, he can gain answers to such questions as: "Does this material provide enough or the right kinds of information for the query I have in mind?" "Is it necessary for me to read the entire chapter or can I read a small section of the material for my purpose?" "Is the book well organized and easily read?" If surveying is practiced by all pupils, the procedure can save them much valuable time in discarding reading matter which is not pertinent to their needs.

Comprehension and effective retention of the basic understandings which may be derived from a set of materials are greatly enhanced by previewing techniques, especially if the pupils are taught to form guiding questions *before* they begin actual reading. Skill in the construction of guiding questions is developed by demonstrations such as the following which are given by the teacher.

A sixth grade class is studying a social studies unit entitled, "Brazil, Land of the Amazon." A textbook which includes a section on the subject is used along with other supplementary books which are written on varying reading levels. One of the books contains a chapter with the following headings:

Name of Chapter: *The Jungle Areas of South America*

Subheadings: 1. The Land Along the Amazon
2. Weather and Climate of the Jungle
3. The Importance of the Amazon Area to the Economy of Brazil
4. Agriculture in the Amazon Basin
5. American Industry Gains a Foothold in the Jungle

The class members have decided that they want to discover the answers to a number of questions. One such question is "What crops are grown in Brazil and are they exported to the United States?" The teacher calls attention to the title of the chapter and asks each pupil to notice the five major subheadings. She then asks: "Which subheadings might contain the information which we are seeking?" The children respond appropriately that subheadings three and four are the most likely to contain the desired answers, and they therefore decide to eliminate the other subheadings from consideration as topics to be read. She also directs the pupils to look at the circle graph on a certain page which denotes the names of the major crops of the Amazon river basin and indicates what portion of the total export trade each of the crops represents. Further attention is also drawn to bar graphs which indicate similar information.

The methods to employ in successfully surveying a chapter or section must be demonstrated in order to convince pupils that the procedure has tremendous value. Provide the pupils with an unfamiliar text and place slips of paper over the title of the chapter and the various subheadings as well as any charts or graphs. Ask them to find the answer to a question which calls for finding a detail or a main idea in a given limited time period. Use another familiar text without covering these sections and ask similar questions. Most children will have discovered the worth of previewing at this point.

This author has found that a sizable number of high school and university students do not use surveying procedures because they have not been taught how to use them or they are not convinced that they have practical value. In one informal study which was completed by this author in late 1966, three out of four university freshmen began reading the very first word of a given chapter and continued throughout the rest of the section without any noticeable regard for previewing the material. If this condition exists in other areas as well, the directive for the elementary, junior high, and senior high teacher in *all* areas is clear. Sequential practical training in this important aspect must be given and such training should be made a natural part of the reading act of each of the pupils. Pupils must be given a clear purpose for reading and be expected to complete many reading assignments which will give them adequate practice in reading for details, reading for main ideas, and reading to find a sequence of events. The act of previewing must be made meaningful to the pupils as early as the first grade and practice on this important skill must be maintained by each succeeding teacher.

Adjusting Reading Rate According to Reading Purpose

Effective reading in the content area is accompanied by a suitable rate of reading which is commensurate with the reader's purpose. After a pupil has previewed a chapter or a section in a text and has developed the guiding questions, he is charged with the responsibility for locating the exact portions which appear to supply the desired information. A number of students may well have developed these desirable habits, but they insist on reading all of these materials at the *same* rate.

Referring to the lesson described earlier concerning the social studies unit on Brazil, assume that the pupil wants to use the source to find the answer to the question, "What American companies have established large factories in Brazil?" The efficient reader will survey the chapter quickly and decide that the answer probably will be found in subheading five and will read slowly, word-by-word, until he has found the answer. On the other hand, if he is seeking an answer to a main idea question such as "Is Brazil a generally wet or dry country?", he would turn to subheading two and read rapidly until he has found the answer to his question.

Since there appears to be a lack of clear understanding among pupils with respect to the importance of reading rate, definite instruction must be given which will allow the individual pupil to decide when he should read at various speeds. For example, one must indicate to the students that skimming is not just a casual, random reading of special materials. After the students have grasped the principles involved in previewing, practice should first be given in having them skim two or three sentences for a specific detail. Later this type of practice should be extended to include longer paragraphs, a page, a unit section, and the entire chapter. A variety of subject matter materials in the areas of science, social studies, literature, and mathematics should be employed. Students making use of these practice procedures must have a particular detail in mind before they make any attempt to skim the material. Flexibility must be employed at all levels of instruction. The difficulty of the materials must be matched with the varying levels of reading competency which are displayed by the different students.

In the effective teaching of reading rate skills, one must stress that reading speed is correlated closely with reading purpose. A large number of reading materials of varying reading difficulty in several subject areas should be used. A list of suggested materials is included in Appendix E of this volume.

Summarizing and Organizing Content Material

Because much of the reading material in the content area is written in a compact style and contains a large number of difficult concepts, many pupils experience difficulty in organizing the content into a meaningful unit of information. There is ample evidence to prove that efficiency in these skills is a powerful aid in comprehending content materials. Even a casual observation by a trained observer reveals that many students at the upper grade and high school levels have not achieved acceptable levels of competency in such skills as arranging sections of a report in the correct order, locating topic sentences, and identifying irrelevant or contradictory statements.

The use of a reading-study formula such as SQ3R (survey, question, read, recite, review) may well be a significant aid to the elementary child in overcoming many of the handicaps associated with the organization of content material.

Pupils should understand that many textbooks in the content areas have study helps such as side headings, center headings, and words, phrases, and sentences which are italicized. They should realize that these devices have been employed by the author to emphasize certain ideas. Additional aids such as questions at the close of the chapter and supplementary reading references should be noted. Difficult concepts should be indicated and explained to the pupils *before* a reading assignment is undertaken. Unless these concepts (especially in social studies and science) are noted, the degree of competency in comprehension will be at a level under that which the student is capable of establishing.

Using and Understanding the Use of Library Facilities

The efficient use of the school library is a skill which is often taken for granted. Many pupils fail to make effective use of the library in content area reading because they fail to understand how the library is arranged, how the Dewey Decimal System has been established, and where and how to use certain reference tools such as encyclopedias, almanacs, dictionaries, and indexes of various kinds.

The final responsibility for training pupils in the effective use of library skills must be the domain of both the teacher and the librarian. If a librarian is not available, then the teacher has the responsibility for such training. Very early in the school year, each pupil (beginning at least at the third grade level) should be given sequential lessons in order that he might understand the following:

1. The physical arrangement of the library including the location of special series of books, instruction in the use of the card catalog, and the relationship and importance of the Dewey Decimal System in locating pieces of requested information.

2. The construction and use of various encyclopedias with particular attention given to the format of the topics, indexes, and special charts and graphs which may be of a unique nature. A similar presentation should be made for almanacs and atlases.

3. The services which are rendered by the school librarian. The librarian should be considered a friend by all children and one who stands ready to help them with different types of reading materials for greater understanding of content area subjects.

READING IN THE SOCIAL STUDIES

At the late third grade level, pupils are asked to read in a variety of content subject areas, particularly those in the social studies. Books in this area oftentimes are quite lengthy and exhibit a frightening image for many pupils. Every good teacher immediately recognizes the situation which confronts these pupils and sets out to provide both intensive and extensive training to make them feel at ease with the materials. The authors of the materials quite often assume that children have had a sufficient background of experiences to comprehend the concepts and ideas which are developed. The content of many books in the social studies is condensed and contains a large number of difficult concepts in a short amount of space. In many instances the materials are of a controversial nature. In the sections which follow, some of the important aspects of reading instruction in the social studies are indicated and some practical activities which may be undertaken to improve each student's skills in these areas are described.

Improving and Enlarging Vocabulary Skills

Since the social studies area contains its own special vocabulary, time must be taken to present the new words and phrases which may be strange and difficult.

In this section several suggestions are given which may be used to develop these skills:

1. Place the new words on the chalkboard and help the pupils understand the correct pronunciation for each word or phrase. Illustrate the meaning of the words and phrases by providing study sheets which contain sentences in which the meanings are clearly indicated. Note, for example, that meanings change from chapter to chapter as in the case of the word, "mandate." Call attention to the fact that the election of a given government official may have been referred to as a "mandate of the people" in a previous chapter, but the word "mandate" in the phrase, "a German mandate" in the present chapter has an entirely different meaning. Unless pupils are alerted to these transitional meanings, they may well form a single meaning and be quite confused when the word is presented in a different context.

2. Another procedure for improving vocabulary is to have children study Latin derivatives, prefixes, and suffixes. Illustrate, for example, the meanings of such prefixes as "mono" and "tri," as in the words "monoplane" and "triangle," in order to establish that "mono" means one and that "tri" means three.

3. Encourage pupils to construct and use a personal file of new vocabulary words which have been encountered. Using his own dictionary, he should indicate the correct pronunciation of each word, the several meanings which the word might have (particularly within the scope of the social studies topics), and how it might be used in a sentence.

4. Serious dictionary study may well be developed around a study topic in social studies. During the study, pupils should be asked to select the one meaning which applies to a particular word found in a contextual situation. Many authors of social studies material provide glossaries which should be used as a major tool in dictionary word study—

in fact, glossaries may well be used as a primary source and the dictionary as a secondary source.

Increasing Comprehension Abilities in Social Studies

Even after each child has understood each of the new words and concepts which may occur in a social studies assignment, the difficult task of assimilating and understanding the total material remains. If he has been stimulated to see sources other than the textbook, he will need to develop skill in locating and evaluating such material in light of the original questions which he developed for the assignment.

The social studies area is a "natural" for the development of several very important skills and understandings in comprehension. At least four of these aspects are noted in the following sections along with suggestions which one might use for the promotion of each:

1. *Reading to develop a concept of sequence of events is an important skill to be learned.* Children must be made to understand that important relationships do exist among events and that a thorough knowledge of these relationships is necessary in order to grasp the global nature of the social sciences. The use of time lines and tables enables the pupils to understand events in history. He is able to see, for example, that World War I took place during the same time that Woodrow Wilson was President and that Nebraska was admitted to the Union during the administration of Andrew Johnson.

2. *Reading to evaluate critically is one of the higher level comprehension skills which is required of pupils.* A critical evaluation of each material is a necessary requirement in a democracy. When pupils are reading from various sources to find pertinent answers to questions in social studies, they must be alerted to make the following mental queries concerning such materials: "When was it written?" "What are the qualifications of the writer?" "Does the author have a particular motive in mind for writing the material?" "How does the material in this source compare with the information I have found in other sources?" "Do I note any propaganda techniques such as name calling, card stacking, and unqualified endorsements in the material?"

3. *Reading graphs, tables, and maps to help understand certain facts in history, geography, and the other social sciences is a vital skill which should be developed by children as early as the primary grades.* Much information can be understood more thoroughly through the use of such devices to convey information.

   In far too many cases pupils tend to ignore such aids as being of insignificant value in comprehending certain concepts. As an illustration of this point, students should be made to understand that the use of bar graphs is an important technique for helping the reader understand, for example, the steady growth in population in the United

States which occurred from 1900 to the present. The proper interpretation of certain maps will help to explain the various altitudes which one might expect to encounter on a trip from St. Louis, Missouri to Fresno, California. When the aids are first introduced in the text, the teacher should explain their proper use by a thorough explanation of the various symbols. The use of the opaque projector to enlarge the device might also help the pupils receive the proper understanding of its value.

READING IN MATHEMATICS

Though not as much reading is normally required in mathematics assignments as in social studies, each pupil must gain competence in the vital areas of vocabulary and comprehension. Some pupils are able to disguise their reading problems in arithmetic as long as they are not confronted with a large number of story-type problems. However, in dealing with story problems, they are forced to understand the meaning of such terms as "ratio," "capital," and "subtrahend," if they are to understand the rationale for the computation processes.

Aiding Vocabulary Skills in Mathematics

Because so many words found in mathematics are found in other subject areas as well, a careful and sequential program of vocabulary development in arithmetic must be undertaken. Suggestions for helping pupils in this area are included in the section which follows:

1. Teach pupils to recognize the differences in words which are commonly found in arithmetic and in other subjects. The word, "principal," for example, has an entirely different meaning when computing problems dealing with loans than when the term is used in referring to various school officials.

2. Alert students to the importance of using the glossary for pronunciation, spelling, and the meaning of such mathematical terms as "percentage," "multiplicand," and "sum."

3. Ask a small group of pupils to construct a continuous bulletin board display of all important words and phrases which denote the origin of the words, together with word families which contain the same root but different prefixes and suffixes and other characteristics.

4. Help students to understand the full meanings of such abbreviations as "mi.," "hr.," "ft.," and "sec." Using the chalkboard, list all of the common abbreviations with their full word opposites. Use a brief teacher-made examination to evaluate each child's competency in this area.

5. After having studied several words and phrases which are relatively new to the pupils, ask each of them to explain a mathematical procedure using all of the words in the explanation.

Helping Children to Understand Word Problems Effectively

Children should be made to understand that they should concentrate primarily on the proper understanding and use of word cues in verbal problems instead of undue emphasis on figures. They should remember, for example, that "part of" may mean to divide and that "difference" means subtract. Other suggestions which might be employed are:

1. Each pupil should be made to understand that in solving problems he must determine (1) what numbers and other facts are given, (2) what kinds of answers he is trying to derive, (3) what arithmetic procedure should be used, and (4) the sequence of the steps to be employed for solving the problem.

2. The value of the slow, careful reading of each problem should be emphasized. While reading, the pupil should concern himself primarily with the basic parts of each sentence, including important word cues and facts and figures which are important ingredients in solving the problem.

3. Give students a list of basic facts and figures and let them construct word problems which will require the reader to use any one of several arithmetical procedures to solve the problems. One should emphasize that all necessary information must be included in each problem if it is to be understood and solved in a reasonable length of time.

4. Encourage the development of the skill in recognizing a sensible answer to a problem. If they feel that the answer is not reasonable, they should be motivated to reread the problem to see if they have failed to read significant parts of the problem.

5. Ask pupils to write the directions for understanding the meaning of certain kinds of mathematical tables. Other students should be requested to read the directions and indicate if they are able to understand the concepts from the directions which have been given.

READING IN SCIENCE

The reading materials to be found in the area of science are in many ways different from those typically found in the social sciences and mathematics. Much of the reading is explanatory rather than narrative in nature and quite often the pupils are confronted with various facts and figures and difficult concepts such as scientific laws and principles.

The efficient reader of science materials should be able to make use of a large number of sources in addition to the regular textbook. He should be able to understand the specialized construction of each source book including the table of contents, glossary, and index. His rate of reading should be adjusted according to the type and difficulty and his purpose for reading. Some types of general material can be read at a rather rapid rate while explanations regarding the conduct of certain types of experiments must be read at a slow, deliberate rate in order to grasp all of the details.

Adequate comprehension of materials in science is quite often difficult for many pupils due to the number of technical terms which are introduced. New words and concepts must be carefully presented and emphasized through the use of graphs, models, charts, and scientific instruments of various kinds. Words, in and by themselves, have no meaning unless some experience is connected with them. The more intense the association with the word, the more meaningful the word becomes for the reader.

Since a large number of reading aids are available in the area of science, each child must develop the skill to evaluate each material intelligently in light of such questions as "How is this material relevant to the problem which I am trying to solve?" "How does the information correlate with similar information found in other books on this subject?" "Is the source book too general or too technical to meet my needs?"

Presenting a Lesson in Science

In meeting the reading needs of students which have been suggested in the previous paragraphs, keep in mind the following steps for presenting a lesson in science (and in other content areas as well):

1. *Developing readiness.* During the readiness period a discussion should take place which would have the pupils recall in various ways the experiences which they have had with the topic or topics under consideration. For example, the children may be asked to describe any experiences which they might have had regarding tornadoes and other types of storms as a preliminary step to the study of weather at the fifth grade level. During the class period any difficult words, phrases, or concepts should be introduced and explained. Questions should be formulated *with* the pupils. As a result of this group effort, the guiding questions for the unit on weather may include some of the following: "What causes tornadoes?" "How are clouds formed?" "What are the most prevalent kinds of precipitation in the mountain states?" These and other questions should serve as the guiding questions for the unit reading. Pupils should be urged to read in many sources other than the textbook for answers to these questions.

2. *Silent Reading.* During the silent reading period, the pupils should read in materials which are on their instructional level. Observe the silent reading habits of each pupil and make proper notes regarding finger pointing, careless reading, and other habits.

3. *Discussion of the topic.* A discussion of the topic should be conducted and should be in terms of the questions which were posed during the readiness period. Opportunity should be given for oral re-reading of certain passages which may be difficult to understand.

4. *Culminating activities and skill development.* In the area of science many worthwhile, interesting activities can take place which are of immense help to the pupils in understanding concepts which are developed in the reading materials. Experiments such as watching small clouds form when steam is placed against cold objects can aid in a child's understanding of how real clouds are formed in the atmosphere. Many children may wish to draw pictures from various cloud formations of a snowstorm. The showing of films and filmstrips on appropriate unit topics can also aid the pupils in forming lasting concepts.

As was the case in the other content subjects, pupils find varying degrees of difficulty in adjusting to the vocabulary which is typically presented in science materials. One cannot develop proficiency and a great scope of understanding unless he is able to master the language of given fields of study. In science materials, a large number of specialized and technical words are typically grouped in a brief paragraph or section of a chapter. Difficulties arise for the young child since many words found in the language of science have entirely different meanings from their everyday uses, as illustrated by the sentence, "The shirt was charged with positive electricity!"

Though most elementary children will not become scientists in the formal sense, they cannot avoid technical or scientific terms if they wish to gain even a passing knowledge of a given topic. The teacher must be careful to sift out these terms and help the pupils deal with them before they become discouraged when they meet them in their reading materials. Motivation is important since the child must see a need for learning the new words and grasp the realization that understanding is only developed after a thorough acquaintance with words is established.

The basic study skills in science require that each pupil has the competency to interpret and analyze scientific symbols and abbreviations and terms which help to explain these aspects. Since many times these concepts are not explained a second time, a cumulative understanding of them is necessary on the part of each child.

Improving Comprehension Skills in Science

In the following section, many suggestions are included for developing the skills of pupils in the area of comprehension of science materials. Each suggestion should be adapted to a given classroom situation in light of the number of pupils enrolled and the grade or ability levels of the pupils involved.

1. List the new words and symbols which are included in the unit on the chalkboard or on a tagboard. Explain the pronunciation and meaning of each new word or symbol. Ask pupils to use these terms in written assignments which are meaningful.

2. Develop crossword puzzles which involve the use of new concepts. Encourage the children to construct similar puzzles and to exchange them with other boys and girls in the class.

3. Call attention to the use of the science glossary as a means of understanding new concepts.

4. Plan a thorough study of different kinds of graphs and charts which appear regularly in the materials. Request the pupils to interpret selected charts and graphs in terms of principles and/or conclusions which might properly be drawn from the plotted information.

5. Conduct chalkboard demonstrations which will help the students to understand scientific formulas. Ask them to explain a given formula in sentence form on a piece of paper. On other occasions, give a written explanation of a principle and ask the pupils to construct a formula which would convey the same information as the written version.

6. Use actual specimens with accompanying pictures and diagrams in order to "clinch" the meaning of certain words such as "aorta" and "pistil."

7. Accompany pupils on field trips to such places as observatories, weather stations, and science laboratories in local high schools and colleges. Brief the person at the location relative to the objectives of the science unit in order that he or she can clarify various points which may be difficult to understand from textbook or other source materials.

8. Invite guest speakers to come to the classroom for demonstrations and explanations of various scientific topics. In studying the unit on weather, a local weather forecaster may explain the principles which he takes into account in making weather predictions. He perhaps can assist the pupils in understanding difficult concepts which they have failed to grasp up to this point.

9. Have selected students perform experiments for the remainder of the class and ask the other students to write an account of the results. This type of exercise checks the student's ability to understand the scientific principles which are being demonstrated.

EVALUATION OF CONTENT AREA READING SKILLS

In order to assess the abilities of each pupil in reading content materials, one should conduct a continuous evaluation. Informal procedures may be used, such as the administration of a list of comprehension questions which have been constructed for a particular selection in a given subject area. The results of such an examination can help determine the common strengths and limitations of individuals for the group as a whole. Those who need specific help can be identified and aided accordingly.

The questions used with the selection should require the pupils to read for details, main ideas, sequence of events, and differences between facts and opinions.

Though evaluation of the pupils is an important aspect of the reading program, the teacher should check himself or herself with regard to teaching practices in this area. The following evaluation sheet may be of much help.

EVALUATION OF TEACHING PRACTICES
RELATED TO READING IN CONTENT AREAS*

Self-evaluation is one technique for the teacher to use in taking stock of how effectively he instructs students in the subjects he teaches. Strengths and weaknesses are pinpointed. The following checklist may be used by an individual or a group of teachers in assessing the extent to which fifteen recommended practices related to reading in the content areas are followed. Direction for school-wide improvement in teaching reading in the content areas may result from an entire faculty using the checklist.

Checklist of Practices Related to Reading in Content Areas

Subject _____ Grade _____ Teacher _____

Directions: The fifteen practices listed below are often recommended in teaching effectively the special reading skills in the various content areas. Indicate the extent to which the practice is being followed in your class. Encircle the appropriate response from among the four given.

1. Text material used is suited in difficulty to the reading levels of students.

   Almost always   Most of the time   Sometimes   Seldom or never

2. Students are encouraged through assignments to read widely in related materials.

   Almost always   Most of the time   Sometimes   Seldom or never

3. At the beginning of the year, adequate time is taken to introduce the text and to discuss how it may be read effectively.

   Almost always   Most of the time   Sometimes   Seldom or never

4. The teacher is aware of the special vocabulary and concepts introduced in the various units.

   Almost always   Most of the time   Sometimes   Seldom or never

5. Adequate attention is given to vocabulary and concept development.

* Reprinted by permission of the author, Dr. Ira Aaron.

Almost always   Most of the time   Sometimes   Seldom or never

6. Provisions are made for checking on the extent to which important vocabulary and concepts are learned and re-teaching is done where needed.

Almost always   Most of the time   Sometimes   Seldom or never

7. The teacher knows the special reading skills involved in the subject.

Almost always   Most of the time   Sometimes   Seldom or never

8. The teacher teaches adequately the special reading skills in the subject.

Almost always   Most of the time   Sometimes   Seldom or never

9. The course content is broader in scope than a single textbook.

Almost always   Most of the time   Sometimes   Seldom or never

10. Assignments are made clearly and concisely.

Almost always   Most of the time   Sometimes   Seldom or never

11. Students are taught to use appropriate reference materials.

Almost always   Most of the time   Sometimes   Seldom or never

12. Adequate reference materials are available.

Almost always   Most of the time   Sometimes   Seldom or never

13. Plenty of related informational books and other materials are available for students who read at below-grade level.

Almost always   Most of the time   Sometimes   Seldom or never

14. Plenty of related informational books and other materials are available for students who read above grade level.

Almost always   Most of the time   Sometimes   Seldom or never

15. The teacher takes advantage of opportunities that may arise to encourage students to read recreational as well as informational reading matter.

Almost always   Most of the time   Sometimes   Seldom or never

Summary

There are a number of difficulties which are involved in reading content area materials at all grade levels. Social science and science materials quite often are written in a compact manner, constructed with a large number of unfamiliar words and concepts, and a number of statements are interspersed which may be controversial in nature.

If pupils are to be efficient in the area of content heading, they must be adept at surveying material, adjusting reading rate, summarizing selections, and understanding the use of library facilities.

Vocabulary and comprehension should be stressed in all content areas through the use of appropriate activities which have been described in this chapter. In each content area, one should develop readiness for the lesson, assign silent reading, discuss the topic, and develop appropriate culminating activities.

Evaluation of the content area reading abilities should be of a continuous nature and should be designed for the benefit of both the pupils and the teacher.

Selected References

1. Bond, Guy L., and Tinker, Miles A. *Reading Difficulties: Their Diagnosis and Correction.* New York: Appleton-Century-Crofts, 1967. Chapter 15.
2. Bond, Guy L., and Wagner, Eva Bond. *Teaching the Child to Read.* New York: The Macmillan Company, 1966. Chapter 13.
3. Dawson, Mildred A., and Bamman, Henry A. *Fundamentals of Basic Reading Instruction.* New York: David McKay Company, Inc., 1959. Chapter 15.
4. Dechant, Emerald. V. *Improving the Teaching of Reading.* Englewood Cliffs, New Jersey: Prentice-Hall, Inc., 1964. Chapter 13.
5. Robinson, H. Alan, and Rauch, Sidney J. *Guiding The Reading Program.* Chicago: Science Research Associates, Inc., 1965. Chapter 7.
6. Smith, Henry P., and Dechant, Emerald V. *Psychology in Teaching Reading.* Englewood Cliffs, New Jersey: Prentice-Hall, Inc., 1961. Chapter 13.
7. Smith, Nila B. *Reading Instruction for Today's Children.* Englewood Cliffs, New Jersey: Prentice-Hall, Inc., 1963. Chapter 10.
8. Spache, George D. *Reading in the Elementary School.* Boston: Allyn and Bacon, Inc., 1964. Chapter 9.
9. Tinker, Miles A., and McCullough, Constance M. *Teaching Elementary Reading.* New York: Appleton-Century-Crofts, Inc., 1962. Chapter 12.
10. Witty, Paul A., Freeland, Alma Moore, and Grotberg, Edith H. *The Teaching of Reading.* Boston: D. C. Heath and Company, 1966. Chapter 10.

8

Applying Current Approaches to Reading Instruction

Since reading is a complex act, every alert teacher should seek to find and to use various methods to teach reading to children of all ages. In employing these procedures, it is necessary for the teacher to understand the basic characteristics of each method in order that she might determine its value in each situation.

To accomplish the goal set forth in the previous sentence, appropriate information is included in this chapter relating to the following approaches: basal materials, linguistic, language-experience, individualized, and the eclectic. In a later part of the chapter some comments have been made relative to such subjects as Words In Color, Initial Teaching Alphabet, programmed reading instruction, mechanical aids, the future of computerized instruction in reading, and needed research in reading. A summary of the total discussion is included at the close of the chapter.

BASAL MATERIALS APPROACH

The approach which is most widely used at the present time is the basal materials approach. Several leading publishers have produced these materials, which usually consist of a set of from six to as many as sixteen basal readers, accompanying workbooks or practice books, teacher manuals, reading readiness materials, reading tests, and other aids. Some companies publish "co-basals" which are designed to complement a regular basal series. The materials are constructed under the direction of one or more reading authorities and are designed to provide a sequential program of reading instruction in such skills as word recognition, vocabulary, and comprehension.

In recent years, much criticism has been directed toward the nature of the stories offered in many of the basal readers. In some cases the stories have not been typical of the experiences encountered by the majority of the pupils, particularly those from culturally disadvantaged environments. Some mention has also been made regarding the restricted vocabulary of many readers. Recently several companies have developed materials which tend to offset these criticisms. Stories now include children from different ethnic and racial groups and the vocabulary has been expanded.

A discussion of basal materials would not be complete without some comment regarding the use of workbooks or practice books which accompany the basal readers. When used properly, the exercises in these books provide proper practice for those children who need reinforcement in certain reading skill areas. Frequently, gross misuse is made of such materials when *all* pupils are asked to complete *all* pages. Pupils should be asked to complete only those exercises which lend needed practice in deficient skill areas.

There are a number of significant advantages in favor of this approach. In nearly all cases the books contain attractive illustrations and are bound in a satisfactory manner. The type used is appropriate for the respective grade levels. A very carefully designed sequence of reading skills is developed throughout the program. Manuals contain a large number of usable ideas for the teacher and thus save much time in planning lessons.

There are few, if any, inherent limitations with respect to the materials. Observed limitations rest with the teacher who may tend to become "manual-bound" and misuse the workbook exercises. When used properly, the basal materials represent an outstanding approach to reading.

THE LINGUISTIC APPROACH TO READING

From a number of aspects the linguistic approach is a difficult approach to explain. The linguist is typically concerned with the structure of language—phonemes, morphemes, prefixes, suffixes. There are several schools of thought in linguistics. George Spache explains the differences in this manner:

> One such school, that of the phonologists, concerns itself with the analysis of the sounds of spoken (and written) language. Leonard Bloomfield is credited by most of his fellow linguists with identification of the various phonemes which are basic sounds of our language. As early as 1942 Bloomfield attempted to outline the implications of this particular linguistic research for reading instruction.
>
> A second school of linguists, sometimes called grammarians or struc-

tural linguists, has investigated the structure of the language. They point out the essential elements of the language that result in the communication of ideas, such as word order or word position, word function, word groups that modify, expand, or change simple expressions, and the signals of intonation, as pitch, stress, and pause. Other areas of structural linguistic research include the identification and frequency of types of sentences (simple statements, demands, requests, questions) and grammatical inflections or word changes to indicate tense and number. It is quite apparent that his approach to language would result in a quite different group of implications for reading instruction than would the work of the phonologists.

A third school concerns itself with the psycholinguistics which involves, among other areas, the identification of the elements of prose style, such as personalization, ornamentation, and abstractness. Although it has resulted in some research that concerns the effect of contextual setting upon word meanings, this school has not, to our knowledge, emphasized the direct implications of its studies for reading instruction.*

For further information concerning the total subject of linguistics, consider Charles Fries' *Linguistics and Reading* (Holt, Rinehart and Winston, 1963), Carl A. Lefevre's *Linguistics and the Teaching of Reading* (McGraw-Hill, 1964), or Pose Lamb's *Linguistics in Proper Perspective* (Charles E. Merrill, 1967). A number of companies including Charles E. Merrill and Science Research Associates have published reading materials from the linguistic point of view.

The linguistic approach brings to mind the large number of variations and irregularities in patterns of spelling. Proponents of the approach have compiled materials and suggestions for the teacher which would help develop regular spelling patterns which can be used in the early stages in teaching symbol-sound relationship.

THE LANGUAGE-EXPERIENCE APPROACH

The language-experience approach to initial instruction in reading utilizes all areas of the language arts in a simultaneous effort. In the early stages of the approach, listening and speaking are emphasized and at a later time reading and writing are inculcated to form a meaningful unit in total language development.

In a typical situation the young children describe events which they have witnessed or experienced at school or at home and the teacher records the stories on the chalkboard or on experience charts. With the use of the discovery method, the pupils soon learn that the process of reading is

* Spache, George D. *Reading in the Elementary School.* Boston: Allyn and Bacon, Inc., 1964, pp. 117–18. Reprinted by permission.

recognizing words on the chalkboard or paper and understanding the meaning of them.

After a set of stories has been collected, the teacher plans a series of lessons which are designed to build vocabulary, increase word recognition skills, and sharpen oral reading ability. When using these competencies, each child is encouraged to engage in independent writing activities. He is now expected to write his own stories instead of dictating them to his teacher. At a later date, he should be able to read from trade books which are written at his instructional level.

Teachers can make use of many of the basic tenets of the approach at every grade level. The language arts intake skills of listening and reading should most certainly be correlated in a meaningful manner with the output skills of speaking and writing. With these procedures each child can come to have a greater facility for identifying the written symbol which stands for the spoken word. Capitalizing on the daily experiences of pupils and making them a part of the instructional program in language arts is both sensible and practical. The language-experience approach is described in detail in Lee and Allen's *Learning to Read Through Experience* (Appleton-Century-Crofts, 1963).

THE INDIVIDUALIZED APPROACH

For decades teachers have been told that they should take each child where they find him and teach him on the basis of his present strengths and limitations. The literature with respect to curriculum practices indicates that a number of serious experiments have been undertaken during this century to individualize the instruction of children in arithmetic, reading, and other areas. Some of these experiments have met with much success while others have been of very limited value.

The influence of Willard C. Olson's philosophy of seeking, self-selection, and pacing has had a great impact on those who have developed the individualized reading approach. He believes that the learner seeks from his environment those experiences and materials which are commensurate with his interests and abilities. The child has a far greater enthusiasm for developing a lasting interest and competency in reading if he is allowed to help choose the stories and materials which are to be read.

There are a number of significant aspects related to the individualized approach. In the section which follows, a description is provided of the materials, the organizational procedures, record keeping, the help groups, and the program in action. (The descriptions which follow are based on the author's observations and the reading of accounts of teachers who have or who are now using the approach. Many modified approaches are also in use at the present time.)

The Materials Needed

Since each pupil should have a sizable number of trade books at his disposal, several books should be available for each child in the classroom. These books should be on a variety of subjects and on varying levels of difficulty. For a fourth grade class, books should be available on the first through the eighth grade levels. If the individualized approach is used, an ample budget must be provided for the materials. The value of the program will not be realized if a limited budget is provided.

Some teachers supplement the trade books with basal readers, workbooks, newspapers, pamphlets and similar aids. If this type of program is chosen, these additional materials must be taken into consideration. Teacher-made worksheets which are used during the skills period will also have to be supplied.

The Organizational Procedures

The execution of details related to an individual reading program demands detailed teacher planning if the program is to succeed. A lazy, lackadaisical teacher who is afraid of work and possible criticism should not consider this approach.

Assuming that a large number of reading materials are available for each child, the critical task for the teacher is the organizational procedures related to the individual interviews which are conducted with each child every few days (usually from one to three times a week). While the rest of the class is engaged in individual reading assignments, a three- to ten-minute individual interview is held with each child at which time the teacher asks the child to read a portion of the book orally and checks his comprehension skill strands. To illustrate how the interviews might be scheduled, assume that a sixth grade teacher has twenty-five pupils enrolled in her class. If the formal reading period is scheduled for sixty minutes per day, five days a week, she would have three hundred minutes per week for the interviews. In this situation she could hold two six-minute or three four-minute sessions with each child each week.

Record Keeping

Careful records must be kept of each child's strengths and limitations with respect to reading skills. A notebook with a section devoted to each child should be used. Each time a conference is held with a pupil, a record is made of the name of the book currently being read, and notations are kept relative to the child's understanding of certain words and the degree of accuracy with which he responded to certain comprehension questions.

Individual assignments involving specially prepared worksheets may be given to the child to complete before the next interview. A student may be assigned to an "ad hoc" help group with other children for help on a particular skill which is troublesome for a common group of pupils. Individual and group assignments should be carefully noted in the record book.

Help Groups

Depending upon the organizational structure, small groups of children are called together either during the developmental reading class period or during another part of the day for sequential skill development lessons and/or corrective reading activities which are designed to overcome a common reading deficiency that was noted during the individual conferences. Some teachers use basal reading materials for these purposes, while worksheets and workbooks or a combination of these materials are used by other teachers. In some programs the pupils work as teams on different assignments.

The Program in Action

The successful teacher using the individualized approach must be resourceful and ambitious. A number of positive statements may be made for this approach. Children are given a chance to work as individuals on their own interest and ability levels and are not held back by slower or faster pupils. They tend to read more books than when they are involved in many other types of programs. Teachers have a chance to get to know their pupils as individuals.

THE ECLECTIC APPROACH

An approach used by a significant number of teachers employs the advantages of all the approaches which have been described thus far. Under this arrangement, the teacher commonly uses basal materials as the core of her instruction. Some attention is given to the study of the language as suggested by the linguistic approach; children are given an opportunity to dictate and read stories as in the language-experience approach, and they are encouraged to read in a large number of trade books on their interest and ability levels as suggested by the teacher employing the individual reading approach.

OTHER CURRENT APPROACHES TO READING INSTRUCTION

At the present time much attention is being given to a number of recently developed materials and techniques for reading instruction. In the section which follows, a brief discussion of Words In Color, Initial Teaching Alphabet, programmed reading instruction, mechanical aids or "hardware," and the future of computerized instruction in reading is provided.

Words In Color

Because only approximately 86 per cent of the words in the English language can be attacked with phonetic analysis procedures, a number of new materials such as Words In Color have been developed in order to make the sounds of word parts regular. The materials and philosophy were developed by Dr. Caleb Gattegno, a British educator, as a result of his work among peoples in Ethiopia, Argentina, and India. He takes the position that, since the Chinese and Amharic languages employ large numbers of characters and yet young children learn to read these languages, it is also possible to provide 200 characters in English and make it a phonetic language through the use of color in a special way.

In light of this philosophy, he has developed a number of charts which employ the use of a different color to stand for the twenty vowel sounds and twenty-seven consonant sounds, regardless of the manner in which the sound is spelled.

A number of school systems in America have started to use the Words In Color materials on an experimental basis. As this volume is published, the results of these experiments are not conclusive enough to provide definitive answers concerning the value of the approach.

Initial Teaching Alphabet

The Initial Teaching Alphabet was invented by Sir James Pitman who started using the method with large numbers of children in England about 1960. Pitman believed that children had difficulty in learning to read because of the gross inconsistencies in the letter-sound relationships in traditional English words. In accordance with this philosophy, he developed forty-four symbols with each symbol representing a single sound. Series of materials have been developed for young children by several companies involving the use of the Initial Teaching Alphabet. After the pupils have completed the exercises in the materials, they are transferred to the traditional orthography.

Teachers and administrators have been concerned about the difficulties involved in transferring the child from the I.T.A. to the traditional orthography. Questions have been raised regarding the number of books and the depth of reading interest which children have when they are accustomed to using the I.T.A. approach.

Several research studies have been completed in recent years with the use of experimental groups using the I.T.A. approach and control groups using the traditional approaches. One of the most objective discussions of the values and limitations of the Words In Color and Initial Teaching Alphabet approaches is contained in Perspectives in Reading No. 5 entitled, *First Grade Reading Programs,* published by the International Reading Association, Box 695, Newark, Delaware, 19711. Additional information regarding the I.T.A., Words In Color and other approaches can be found in Jeanne Chall's *Learning to Read: The Great Debate,* published by McGraw-Hill Book Company.

Programmed Reading Instruction

Positive learning can take place in many subject areas, including reading skills through the use of educational aids which divide a large body of skills into small units which can be grasped in a short amount of time. A learning principle is explained and illustrated and the learner is asked to complete a series of exercises which are designed to establish the principle in the learner's mind. The pupil can check immediately to see if he has answered each question; thus immediate reinforcement is available.

Using work sheets, tablets, cards, workbooks, and textbooks, several leading companies have published programs for learning word analysis skills. Each child works independently and progresses at his own rate. The use of the materials can serve to free the teacher from individual drill lessons which are time-consuming. While many aspects of the reading act can be programmed, a number of them cannot. Teachers should experiment with a particular commercial program which is available to discover firsthand what advantages the materials might have for certain pupils.

All programmed materials are not of the "software" variety. Some teaching machines of the "hardware" type are now available which necessitate the child pulling a knob, turning a crank, or pushing a lever or button to record a response. An adequate number of research studies have not been completed which would supply definitive answers regarding the advantages and limitations of such instruments.

Mechanical Aids

A number of companies have been and are presently producing mechanical aids of the tachistoscopic and reading pacer varieties which are designed to increase speed of word recognition and overall rate of reading. Such "hardware" can be effective *if it is used properly with certain children.* There is no machine which, when plugged into an electrical outlet, will remediate serious word recognition problems. The employment of machines for use with certain disabled readers is open to question.

For the *average* and *above average* reader who has a good foundation in word recognition and comprehension skills, mechanical aids may be used, for example, to increase rate of reading. However, the retention of such increases at a later date when machines are not available is debatable. They are used more profitably with upper grade pupils and those at the high school levels.

Due to the expense of such aids, serious thought should be given before wholesale purchases of them are made for developmental and remedial programs where they may be of limited help. For a complete description of the different kinds of mechanical devices, consult Chapter 14 of Emerald Dechant's *Improving the Teaching of Reading.* (Prentice-Hall, Inc., 1964).

Computerized Instruction in Reading

As of 1969, there is considerable discussion concerning the future role of computers for individualized instruction in reading. Computers can be built which will help pupils on an individual basis to learn a body of skills relating to word perception, comprehension, and listening. They can be of great aid to the reading clinician in the diagnosis of reading difficulties, since they may be able to classify and catalogue the exact kinds of oral reading difficulties, word recognition deficiencies, and other information.

If the cost of computers can be at a level which would allow a large number of schools to purchase them, such instruments may well revolutionize developmental and remedial reading procedures in the 1970's. Teachers would do well to keep apprised concerning the progress of development of these aids and make use of them in their respective schools if they seem applicable to their needs.

NEEDED RESEARCH IN READING

A writer of a volume on reading instruction would be remiss if a discussion were not included concerning the issues in reading which are in urgent need of intensive research. No one area of the elementary school curriculum has been studied more than reading, and yet many unanswered questions remain regarding several significant issues. Many emotional opinions, both written and oral, have been given in the debate on certain topics. Every reader of this work is encouraged to renew his or her efforts in the attempt to find possible solutions to the questions enumerated in the next paragraph. The results of such studies should be published in appropriate journals in order that the entire profession may benefit from the findings.

The following questions constitute significant issues which are yet to be resolved. (While this author is well aware that a number of studies of varying quality have been conducted in each of the areas, the answers to the questions are far from being unequivocal.)

1. What is the best method of grouping children for reading instruction in order that individual differences might be met in an effective manner?

2. Is the code emphasis approach more profitable than a combination code emphasis–whole word approach or a strict whole word approach?

3. To what degree do commercial multi-level reading materials (boxed and book series varieties) meet the reading needs of individual pupils?

4. Do teachers, as a group, provide enough sequential and direct training in the area of listening skills?

5. Of what value are mechanical devices in producing lasting results with regard to rate of reading?

6. Does lateral dominance have a positive relationship to success in reading?

7. To what degree do the common commercial reading tests evaluate the true reading status of culturally disadvantaged pupils?

8. How can dyslexia be diagnosed and what is its effect on reading ability?

Some information relating to these and other questions is now available through a recent nationwide comprehensive information system (Educational Research Information Center) which has been created by the U. S. Office of Education for the acquisition of materials and research reports related to reading and other instructional areas. The National reading clearinghouse has been established at Indiana University and is a joint project of the U.S. Office of Education, the International Reading Association, and Indiana University. The submission of documents and inquiries regarding purchase of materials should be addressed to Eric Crier, 200 Pine Hall, School of Education, Indiana University, Bloomington, Indiana 47401.

The magazines listed in Appendix D very often contain research articles in the area of reading. In addition to these journals, readers may wish to consult *Dissertation Abstracts, The Reading Research Quarterly,* and *The Journal of Educational Research* for information relative to research projects in reading.

Summary

There are a number of significant approaches to reading which are being used in the schools of America. These approaches include basal materials, linguistic, language-experience, individualized, and eclectic. All of these procedures have advantages and limitations and each should be studied carefully before it is incorporated in the philosophy of a given school system.

In addition to these approaches a number of schools have used Words In Color, Initial Teaching Alphabet, programmed reading materials and various mechanical aids to increase reading efficiency. Many of these materials and methods are in the experimental stages and definitive uses and values of them are still in serious question. Computerized instruction is appearing on the educational horizon and may have considerable impact on developmental and remedial reading instruction.

One must remember that the classroom teacher is the key to good reading instruction. Ineffective teachers will remain ineffective even though they may be surrounded by large amounts of new teaching materials of the "hardware" and "software" varieties.

There are many significant questions in the area of reading instruction which are in need of intensive research. Improved techniques will accrue when these questions have been at least partially resolved. Many important sources of information are available to the teacher for the study of research reports.

Selected References

1. Bond, Guy L., and Wagner, Eva Bond. *Teaching the Child to Read.* New York: The Macmillan Company, 1966. Chapter 5.
2. DeBoer, John J., and Dallmann, Martha. *The Teaching of Reading.* New York: Holt, Rinehart and Winston, Inc., 1964. Chapter 12.
3. Dechant, Emerald V. *Improving the Teaching of Reading.* Englewood Cliffs, N.J.: Prentice-Hall, Inc., 1964. Chapter 14.
4. Durr, William K. (Editor). *Reading Instruction: Dimensions and Issues.* Boston: Houghton Mifflin Company, 1967. Chapters 3, 6, 9, 10, 12.
5. Fries, Charles C. *Linguistics and Reading.* New York: Holt, Rinehart and Winston, Inc., 1963.
6. Hunt, Lyman C. (Editor). *The Individualized Reading Program: A Guide for Classroom Teaching.* Proceedings of the International Reading Association, Volume II, Part 3. Newark, Delaware: International Reading Association, 1967.
7. Lamb, Pose. *Linguistics in Proper Perspective.* Columbus, Ohio: Charles E. Merrill Publishing Company, 1967.
8. Lee, Dorris M. and Allen, R. V. *Learning to Read Through Experience.* New York: Appleton-Century-Crofts, 1963.
9. Lefevre, Carl A. *Linguistics and the Teaching of Reading.* New York: McGraw-Hill, 1964.
10. Smith, Nila B. *Reading Instruction for Today's Children.* Englewood Cliffs, N.J.: Prentice-Hall, Inc., 1963. Chapters 5, 7.
11. Spache, George D. *Reading in the Elementary School.* Boston: Allyn and Bacon, Inc., 1964. Chapters 3, 4, 5, 6.

9

Evaluating the Reading Program

In order to assess the degree to which the adopted objectives of a reading program are being met, various evaluative devices and techniques must be developed. The total program must be a joint endeavor with all members of the school staff participating in the selection of tools and the manner in which they are to be employed. The reading program should be revised in light of the results obtained from the evaluative procedures.

In order to secure a basic understanding of a thorough program, the purposes of evaluation, types of evaluative tools, factors to consider in test selection and administration, the interpretation of evaluative instruments, and basic principles of instruction for the retarded and gifted reader are discussed in this chapter.

THE PURPOSES OF EVALUATION

If the reading curriculum is to be improved, one must keep in mind that the systematic use of both standardized and informal measures on both a periodic and continuous basis will be necessary. Careful selection of such tools in accordance with predetermined reading objectives must be undertaken.

The first purpose of evaluation is the attempt to ascertain the degree to which formulated reading objectives are being met. For example, if one of the major reading goals at the intermediate grade level is the development of efficient reading of maps and graphs, and results from tests indicate a pronounced deficiency in this area, it reveals to the school authorities that a greater degree of emphasis must be placed in the development of this objective. In far too many cases, standardized tests are administered in a ritualistic manner without regard to their implications for the school reading program. The proper use of these results should cause teachers and administrators to make necessary changes in the methods and materials employed in reading classes.

The second major purpose of evaluation is to acquire knowledge relative to the reading strengths and limitations of students, both individually and collectively. A survey test may well be administered to the total school population in order to identify those pupils who need more intensive diagnosis and extended remedial services. Individual diagnostic instruments may be used to identify the specific limitations of pupils in such areas as vocabulary, comprehension, word analysis, and oral reading. The information derived from such procedures should be a significant consideration in building a sound program of remedial reading activities for the retarded reader.

TYPES OF EVALUATIVE TOOLS

All evaluative instruments can generally be classified as being either standardized or informal. Both types should be used extensively but prudently. A discussion of the role of each is included in the following sections.

Standardized Tests

Standardized tests in reading can be classified under the following headings: survey, diagnostic, oral, and reading readiness. Many of these tools can be used as either individual or group tests, while others are strictly individual in nature.

Among other purposes, *SURVEY* tests serve as formal devices for evaluating the general objectives of a reading program and gaining an impression of group reading abilities. Survey tests in and by themselves are not designed to give a detailed summary of any student's reading capabilities; however, they can be used to identify those pupils who need intensive individual diagnosis. A large number of the tests attempt to measure such aspects as reading vocabulary, sentence or paragraph comprehension, and reading speed. Norms for the tests are established typically from regional and nation-wide testing, and any given student's score is interpreted in terms of grade scores or percentiles. Many local school authorities wisely compile local norms which may be more realistic standards for interpreting scores of pupils from particular schools.

The tests mentioned in the following section are representative of the kinds of survey tests used in some schools for the purposes previously discussed.

The *Botel Reading Inventory* (one form for Grades 1-12) evaluates phonics mastery, word recognition, reading, listening, and word comprehension (Follett Publishing Company).

Comprehensive Tests of Basic Skills (two forms for each of four levels for use from grades 2.5-12) evaluate reading vocabulary and comprehension as well as language mechanics, expression, and spelling (California Test Bureau).

Gates-MacGinitie Reading Tests (three forms of nine tests are available for use from Grades 1-12) check speed, comprehension, and vocabulary (Teachers College Press, Columbia University).

Iowa Every-Pupil Tests of Basic Skills (four forms available for Grades 3-9) surveys ability in such areas as vocabulary and paragraph comprehension, reading graphs, charts, tables, and maps, as well as use of references, index, dictionary, and alphabetizing (Houghton-Mifflin).

Stanford Achievement Test: Reading (three to five forms for Grades 2-9) checks paragraph and word meaning (Harcourt, Brace and World).

SRA Achievement Series: Reading (one or two forms for Grades 1-9) surveys such areas as language perception, comprehension, vocabulary, and work-study skills (Science Research Associates).

DIAGNOSTIC tests are designed primarily to lend valuable detailed information to the teacher or clinician regarding a given child's abilities in oral reading, word analysis skills, visual and auditory discrimination of letters, spelling, listening, along with data concerning his instructional, frustration, and potential reading levels. To be of greatest value, diagnostic tests should be administered as individual tests by those who have had at least a minimum of formal clinical training. The results of such instruments must be the object of careful study in order to avoid misunderstanding regarding the true strengths and limitations of a given child.

In the following paragraphs several standardized diagnostic tests which can be used in school and clinic situations are discussed.

Diagnostic Reading Scales (one form individual test for Grades 1-6 and older retarded readers) analyzes sight-word vocabulary, word analysis techniques, oral reading, and silent reading comprehension (California Test Bureau).

Doren Diagnostic Reading Test (one form group test for Grades 1-9) lends aid relative to a given child's ability in the following skills: letter recognition, beginning sounds, whole word recognition, words within words, speech consonants, ending sounds, blending, rhyming, vowels, and sight words (American Guidance Service, Inc.).

Durrell Analysis of Reading Difficulty (one form individual test for Grades 1-6) evaluates oral reading, silent reading comprehension, listening comprehension, word recognition and word analysis, letters, visual memory of words, sounds, and visual memory of words, spelling, and handwriting (Harcourt, Brace & World).

Gates-McKillop Reading Diagnostic Tests (two forms individual test for Grades 1-8) diagnoses subject's ability in such areas as oral reading, knowledge of word parts, recognizing the visual form of sounds, auditory blending, and supplementary tests in spelling, oral vocabulary, syllabication, and auditory discrimination (Teachers College Press, Columbia University).

Standardized *ORAL* reading tests are constructed to yield significant information relative to a subject's general grade equivalent rating, rate of reading comprehension, and the degree to which he mispronounces, omits, inserts, substitutes, repeats, or inverts words when he reads a series of paragraphs which are prepared at varying levels of difficulty. While the *Diagnostic Reading Scales,* the *Durrell Analysis of Reading Difficulty,* and *Gates-McKillop Reading Diagnostic Tests* have oral reading subsections, the two most widely used standardized measures which are devoted entirely to oral reading analyses are the *Gray Oral Reading* and *Gilmore Oral Reading Tests.* Both of these instruments are described in the following paragraphs.

Gilmore Oral Reading Test (two forms individual test for Grades 1-8) provides accuracy, comprehension, and rate scores and a total grade equivalent. Ample space is allocated for the examiner to make note of substitutions, mispronunciations, insertions, hesitations, repetitions, and omissions. New normative data involving an extensive 1967 standardization population along with color coded tests and accessories are now available. (Harcourt, Brace and World).

Gray Oral Reading Test (four forms individual test for grades 1-12) yields rate, comprehension, and grade equivalent scores and space is provided for noting the types of errors made by the subject. An observation list is also included which allows the examiner to make note of such items as poor phrasing, monotonous tone, poor enunciation, overuse of phonics, head movement, finger pointing, and loss of place (Bobbs-Merrill Company, Inc.).

READING READINESS tests are designed to lend aid to the primary teacher or the clinician in determining to what extent a given child may succeed in the formal reading program. A description of several of these tests is included in Chapter 2 of this volume.

Informal Tests

Informal or subjective measures can be used to screen a group of pupils in order to find information relative to their reading rate and comprehension. A pertinent selection of four or five pages can be duplicated and handed to the pupils for silent reading. As each child finishes, he raises his hand and thus the teacher can identify the slow and fast readers. The response to a brief comprehension test relating to the selection will give some indication with respect to this factor.

The subjective reading inventory can be easily constructed and is an excellent means for determining the frustration, instructional, and potential reading levels of individual pupils. The directions for compiling the instrument are found in Chapter 1.

The administration of informal reading interest inventories can help the teacher to get acquainted with each child and how he feels about reading. The following inventory has been used by this author with many children.

READING INTEREST INVENTORY

1. Name _____ Age _____ Grade _____

2. From what source do you secure most of your free reading books?

   Friends _____ School Library _____ Community Library _____

   Church Library _____

3. How many books have you borrowed during the past month? _____

   How many of the books did you read completely? _____

   Give the titles of some of the books. _____

   _____

4. Check the kinds of books which you like to read.

   Fiction _____ Mysteries _____ Sports _____ Romance _____

   Heroes _____ History _____ Science _____

5. What kinds of hobbies do you have? _____

   _____

6. List the names of three television programs you like best. _____

   _____

7. Give a list of the states and countries which you have visited. _____

   _____

8. Mention the names of three of your favorite newspapers. _____

   _____

9. Which of the following sections of the newspaper do you usually read?

   A. National and local news _____   D. Editorials _____

   B. Comics _____   E. Sports _____

C. Feature stories _____   F. Other _____

10. If you had at least two hours a day to devote to free reading, what kinds of material would you probably select? Why?

_____

_____

_____

_____

The Basic Sight Word Test is an excellent informal test for evaluating a child's ability in the area of sight word recognition. The test, consisting of 220 words which was devised many years ago by Dr. Edward Dolch, is available from the Garrard Publishing Company. Children who have completed the third grade should be able to recognize all words with ease.

A brief subjective spelling test can be made by selecting a few words which are commonly found in various reading and spelling materials at each of several grade levels. Since some studies have shown that the correlation between spelling and reading ability is significant, the assessment of a child's ability in each of these areas is important and necessary.

FACTORS TO CONSIDER IN TEST SELECTION AND ADMINISTRATION

Since there are literally dozens of standardized tests which might well be used in reading evaluation, the selection of appropriate tests for a given group of pupils is no small task. There are several criteria, however, which should be definitely employed in order to avoid haphazard methods.

Guidelines for Choosing Tests

The *objectivity* of a test relates to the amount of individual interpretation which must be given as to the correctness of individual answers. A test which has a high objectivity rating is one which is so built that only one answer can be considered correct for each of the questions.

Test administration and checking are practical aspects which should be judged. Busy teachers who have a minimum of time for formal test administration must not be hampered by complicated instruments. The choice of a survey test may well be governed by the availability of machine scoring.

Pupils respond better to an instrument if the *type size* and *test layout* are both suitable and easy to follow. The *price* of tests must be a practical consideration since the total cost of standardized instruments for a large school system may be a sizable amount.

Validity (the degree to which a given standardized test measures what it is supposed to measure) and *reliability* (the degree to which a test is consistent in its accuracy) are important factors in test selection. Objective comments relating to individual tests can be found in *Reading Tests and Reviews* which is edited by Oscar K. Buros and published by The Gryphon Press.

Test selection should be undertaken by a committee consisting of such persons as classroom teachers, principals, supervisors, and reading consultants. One person should not be given the sole responsibility for this important facet of the evaluation program, since many different persons are involved in the administration and scoring of tests in typical school situations.

Criteria for Administration of Tests

If scores from test instruments are to be valid and useful, certain factors must be a part of the total program of test administration. Careful attention should be given to the statements which follow:

1. The physical surroundings of the classroom must be suitable with regard to comfortable furniture, suitable temperature, and adequate ventilation. Pupils should not be placed in close proximity to each other for reasons of comfort and to lessen the temptation to "borrow" answers.

2. Consideration should be given to the length of the testing periods. A number of short testing periods are much more desirable than are single periods of long duration.

3. The image of the test administrator must radiate a feeling of ease rather than the impression that a given pupil's reputation may well be geared to the results of a test.

4. The examiner must be prepared for the test administration periods. To be properly prepared one must understand all aspects of the test, including time limits, response procedures, and scoring. The results of a test may be invalidated if laxness is tolerated or encouraged.

5. Some explanation should be given to the pupils relative to the purpose of tests. Pupils have a right to know this type of information.

INTERPRETATION OF EVALUATIVE INSTRUMENTS

The area of test interpretation is probably one of the most misunderstood segments of the evaluation program. One should remember these significant principles when interpreting test scores:

1. No one test can determine precisely the reading capabilities of any given pupil. Any one test score should be supplemented with data

derived from other standardized and informal devices as well as the astute observation of the teacher.

2. The reading grade placement derived from many reading achievement tests must be considered a frustration score; thus a pupil's true instructional grade level would be about one grade below that score. His independent reading level may well be two grade levels below the test score level.

3. The degree to which a pupil guesses on a test can never be accurately judged. This factor is especially significant with respect to reading tests employing the use of multiple-choice questions. Three pupils may well receive similar scores on a test, but these scores do not necessarily indicate that these pupils are at the same level of competency in reading skills.

4. One must remember that there are some aspects of the reading process which cannot be evaluated accurately by standardized tests. Among these factors would be critical reading, reading interests, and the use of context clues.

5. Final judgments regarding the reading status of a given pupil should be determined on the basis of comparisons of scores on various tests. If a child scores at a high level in one skill on several tests and at a low level on other skills, one can draw definite conclusions; however, a mixed pattern of scores indicates that further observation and testing is necessary before conclusions are drawn.

BASIC PRINCIPLES OF INSTRUCTION FOR THE RETARDED AND GIFTED READER

While a majority of pupils can be expected to be reading at or near grade level, test results and careful observation frequently reveal a substantial number of pupils who are retarded in reading and a lesser number who are accomplished readers. Assuming that a careful evaluation has been conducted for these pupils, the next most important task is to devise a reading program which will take care of the needs of these pupils who deviate significantly from the norm. In this section, some of the principles to observe in dealing with these kinds of pupils are discussed.

The Retarded Reader

Any child whose reading instructional level is below that of his grade level can be properly classified as a retarded reader. Those pupils who are reading at two or more levels below grade level should be placed in environments where special remedial instruction is possible. Usually this type of instruction is conducted outside of the regular classroom.

If one is to realize a reasonable amount of success in dealing with these kinds of pupils, a number of important considerations must be kept in mind.

1. Instruction for these children must be highly organized. After studying the test scores and other data, a careful outline should be made of the types of exercises and materials available which will serve to alleviate the existing deficiencies of the pupil. The child who shows a haphazard pattern of success in reading is in need of a carefully structured program where a sequence of learning activities is in evidence.

2. The pupil must be able to realize at least a limited amount of success during the treatment process. The old saying, "nothing builds success like success" is certainly true with respect to the reading retardate. Typically, these students are older and have met a long series of defeats and are convinced that they cannot be successful in the area of reading. One must be optimistic and call attention to each bit of improvement registered by the pupil, regardless of how small the improvement might be. A pleasant atmosphere should always pervade and a relaxed situation should be in evidence. Building the confidence of these children may well be one of the most important tasks.

3. A variety of materials and exercises should be employed which are commensurate with a given student's reading needs. Due to the complexity of the reading act, no one set of materials or exercises is so complete that it will suffice for all needs. These children demand the different—the unusual—if their attention is to be captured. The use of informal, homemade devices may be of more value than highly sophisticated commercial gadgets and books. The teacher should not keep changing materials for the mere sake of change. Stay with one program long enough to give it a fair trial.

4. Close cooperation between parent and teacher is absolutely essential in remedial teaching situations. Parents have a perfect right to know what the instructor is doing and why certain provisions are being made for their children. A careful explanation should be made to the parents of these children relative to the reasoning employed in selecting the pupils for the program. A discussion should also be conducted regarding the specific and general objectives which are to be followed in each case. Periodic conferences should be scheduled with the parents in order that they might be properly informed concerning each pupil's progress.

5. The psychological structure of each pupil should be studied as much as possible with the help of qualified persons who can administer various psychological tests. Many retarded readers have poor self-concepts and have a low estimate of their personal worth. Gaining the child's loyalty and confidence should be one of the first jobs. Unfortunately, some of these children have been made the object of ridicule by other children and even by their parents in some cases. The remedial teacher must try to help erase this image.

6. Careful selection of pupils for the remedial programs should be undertaken by both administrators and teachers. Pupils selected should possess at least a low average intelligence as measured by individual tests which have been administered by qualified examiners. Pupils who are in the educable mentally retarded category are in need of special instruction apart from the usual techniques employed by remedial reading teachers. At *no* time should the remedial reading room be a "dumping ground" for pupils who are unruly or who are emotionally disturbed.

7. A remedial program must be viewed by the pupils as an opportunity rather than as a punishment. Pupils should not be purposely removed from enjoyable activities and "sent" to remedial reading lessons.

8. Continuous evaluation should be in evidence at all times. Reading growth in the various reading skill areas should be a constant aid to the teacher in making decisions relating to materials and techniques which appear to be of most value for a given child.

The Gifted Reader

One of the most neglected segments of the school population is that group of pupils who are classified as gifted or bright. Since they are already reading above grade level, many teachers feel that they don't need urgent attention and therefore the teacher's energies are directed toward the retarded readers. If the truly gifted child is not challenged, he may become disinterested and later become a discipline problem. These children need as much of the teacher's time and attention as do the normal or subnormal children. The following suggestions may be of help in working with these kinds of pupils:

1. A distinctive creative approach must be used. One can be more permissive in the assignments which are given. These pupils are much more apt to ask questions and see the reasons behind the methods used by the teacher.

2. A large amount of reading materials in many different areas must be available to provide for the wide range of reading interests which are so characteristic of these pupils. Books should be selected from the school library and public libraries. Paperback selections which are available from various book stores may also be made a part of the total room collection.

3. In some schools, special classes for gifted children have been organized as in the case of the Joplin Plan. Children who are placed in these groups are not to be thought of as being homogeneous in nature, since individual differences among the pupils still exist. The plan does provide for a special means whereby attention is given directly to these children.

4. Several school officials have adopted a policy of acceleration for gifted children. There is some question relating to the possible social problems which may develop as a result of such a procedure. However, this writer's candid observation would suggest that social problems which may be associated with such a program have been grossly exaggerated.

Summary

The two major purposes of an effective program of reading evaluation are to ascertain the degree to which formulated reading objectives are being met and to acquire knowledge relative to the reading strengths and limitations of students, both individually and collectively. The use of both standardized and informal devices should be employed.

Standardized reading tests are classified as either survey, diagnostic, oral, or reading readiness and are designed for use as individual or group measures. Numerous informal tests such as subjective reading inventories, reading interest inventories, and sight word tests may be used as adjuncts to the standardized testing instruments.

Several factors such as ease of scoring, validity, reliability, cost, printing and format should be important considerations in the selections of tests. The interpretation of the instruments should be made with care and in accordance with the principles which have been discussed in this chapter.

Since the program of evaluation will reveal the fact that a sizable percentage of a given school population will be both retarded and advanced, provisions must be made for a sound program of reading instruction for these children.

Selected References

1. Anderson, Verna D. and others. *Readings in the Language Arts.* New York: The Macmillan Company, 1968. Chapters 1 and 7.
2. Barbe, Walter B. *Educator's Guide to Personalized Reading Instruction.* Englewood Cliffs: Prentice-Hall, Inc., 1961. Chapter 5.
3. Bond, Guy L. and Tinker, Miles A. *Reading Difficulties: Their Diagnosis and Correction.* New York: Appleton-Century-Crofts, 1967. Chapters 7, 8, 9, 10.
4. Dawson, Mildred A., and Bamman, Henry A. *Fundamentals of Basic Reading Instruction.* New York: David McKay Company, Inc., 1963. Chapter 16.
5. DeBoer, John J. and Dallmann, Martha. *The Teaching of Reading.* New York: Holt, Rinehart and Winston, Inc., 1964. Chapter 13.
6. Dechant, Emerald V. *Diagnosis and Remediation of Reading Disability.* West Nyack, N.Y.: Parker Publishing Company, Inc., 1968.
7. Heilman, Arthur W. *Principles and Practices of Teaching Reading.* Columbus, Ohio: Charles E. Merrill Books, 1967. Chapter 15.

8. Russell, David H. *Children Learn to Read.* New York: Ginn and Company, 1961. Chapter 16.
9. Schell, Leo M. and Burns, Paul C. *Remedial Reading: An Anthology of Sources.* Boston: Allyn & Bacon, 1968. Part III.
10. Smith, Henry P. and Dechant, Emerald. *Psychology in Teaching Reading.* Englewood Cliffs, N.J.: Prentice-Hall, Inc., 1961. Chapter 15.
11. Smith, Nila B. *Reading Instruction for Today's Children.* Englewood Cliffs, N.J.: Prentice-Hall, Inc., 1963. Chapter 16.
12. Tinker, Miles A. and McCullough, Constance. *Teaching Elementary Reading.* New York: Appleton-Century-Crofts, 1962. Chapter 16.
13. Witty, Paul A., Freeland, Alma, and Grotberg, Edith H. *The Teaching of Reading.* Boston: D. C. Heath and Company, 1966. Chapter 17.

10

The Elementary Teacher and Federally Funded Reading Programs

In 1965, Congress passed a bill which provides for substantial amounts of money for the improvement of instruction at both the elementary and secondary levels. The Elementary and Secondary Education Act, with its five titles, has particular importance with respect to reading instruction, since many new and innovative reading programs have been instituted which have involved hundreds of classroom teachers and school administrators. There is every indication that such involvement will continue and possibly increase in the future.

Limited amounts of professional material have been published which help teachers in understanding their role in these programs. To lend assistance in this important area, the following topics are included in this chapter: a brief summary of the Elementary and Secondary Act of 1965, guidelines for establishing effective reading programs, and the projected role of the Federal government in future elementary reading programs.

THE ELEMENTARY AND SECONDARY EDUCATION ACT OF 1965

Public Law 89-10, more commonly known as the Elementary and Secondary Education Act of 1965, is one of the most significant acts relating to the improvement of education up to this time. The five major titles of the act are as follows: Title I—Financial assistance to local educational agencies for the education of children of low-income families; Title II—Financial assistance for school library resources, textbooks, and other instructional materials; Title III—Provision for financial aid for supplementary educational centers and services; Title IV—Educational research and training financial grants; and Title V—Grants to strengthen state departments of education. (For a complete description of the Act, the reader is encouraged to read a copy of the original document.)

The provisions under Titles I, III, and V have allowed for the establishment of many new programs for the improvement of reading instruction. The largest amount of money has been made possible for school districts which have sizable numbers of children from low-income families. Some districts have received as much as $700,000 under Title I during a given school year for such projects as after school remedial programs in reading, and reading materials such as supplementary reading books, workbooks, and mechanical aids. These aids have been of considerable assistance to teachers, since many districts would not have had the necessary local funds to make such purchases.

Under Title III a large number of innovative reading programs have been made possible. Reading clinics and reading centers for serving both disabled and gifted readers have been established in many cities. An example of a Title III project is the Central Reading Clinic of the Omaha Public Schools (Mr. Ron Meyer, Director) which was made possible by a grant in early 1966. A section of a former elementary school was remodeled for use as a diagnostic and service center for retarded readers who attend either public or private schools. Several client rooms were formed, a video tape machine and television camera were installed for teacher training purposes, and books and tests were purchased for the use of the clients. Since the school system did not previously have such a service, the establishment of this facility greatly aided the opportunities available for retarded readers.

Under Title V, some grants have been made to state departments of education for educational planning of reading programs on a statewide basis and for the employment of reading consultants who can be of service to local school districts. There are a number of other possibilities for state department improvement with respect to reading and other areas encompassed in Title V.

GUIDELINES FOR ESTABLISHING EFFECTIVE READING PROGRAMS

Because sums of money have been made available to various school districts for special reading programs and services, some administrators have tried to develop such innovations in the shortest possible time, and as a result many mistakes have been made. The following guidelines have been constructed to lend insight in the formation of new programs and services.

1. *Survey the reading needs of the district carefully in order to ascertain precisely what kinds of programs are needed.* Such a survey would entail the use of questionnaires, interviews, and in-service meetings

with teachers to determine if the proposed program would be developmental, corrective or remedial in nature. Survey reading tests should be administered to gain some impression of the general reading levels of the pupils to ascertain the need for remedial programs. The proposal for a new program must, and should, be a joint effort of teachers, administrators, boards of education, and in some instances, the parents. A proposal based on the notions of one or two persons is to be deplored.

2. *Analyze the amount of space which is available for new programs.* In order to execute a carefully devised remedial program, adequate space is necessary. Rather than converted broom closets, these rooms should contain at least sixteen square feet for each child who will be using the room. The rooms selected should be well lighted and airy, conducive to fulfillment of the objectives pursued in the reading program.

3. *Secure qualified teachers for the reading program.* The use of unqualified teachers is probably one of the gravest limitations of many programs now in operation. The teaching of reading calls for persons with the highest possible level of training. If such teachers are not already in the school system or cannot be employed for other reasons, the formation of special reading programs might well be delayed until qualified teachers can be found. In order to prevent the hiring of unqualified teachers for newly established reading activities, the International Reading Association has formulated minimum standards for the professional training of reading specialists. All persons who purport to be reading specialists should be able to meet these standards.

Minimum Standards for Professional Training of Reading Specialists*

A. A minimum of three years of successful teaching and/or clinical experience.

B. A Master's Degree with a major emphasis in reading or its equivalent of a Bachelor's Degree plus 30 graduate hours in reading and related areas as indicated below:

(1) A minimum of 12 semester hours in graduate level reading courses with at least one course in each of the following:

(a) Foundations or survey of reading
A basic course whose content is related exclusively to reading instruction or the psychology of reading. Such a course ordinarily would be the first in a sequence of reading courses.

(b) Diagnosis and correction of reading disabilities
The content of this course or courses includes the following: causes of reading disabilities; observation and interview procedures; diagnostic instruments; standard and informal tests; report writing; materials and methods of instruction.

* Reprinted by permission of the International Reading Association.

       (c) Clinical or laboratory practicum in reading

           A clinical or laboratory experience which might be an integral part of a course or courses in the diagnosis and correction of reading disabilities. Students diagnose and treat reading disability cases under supervision.

  (2) An additional minimum of 12 semester hours from the following courses:

       (a) Measurement and/or evaluation

       (b) Child and/or adolescent psychology or development

       (c) Personality and/or mental hygiene

       (d) Educational psychology

       (e) Literature for children and/or adolescents

       (f) Organization and supervision of reading programs

       (g) Research and the literature in reading

       (h) Linguistics

       (i) Communications

       (j) Curriculum

  (3) The remainder of semester hours from additional courses listed above and/or related areas such as:

       (a) Foundations of education

       (b) Guidance

       (c) Speech and hearing

       (d) Exceptional child

4. *Use materials from a variety of sources.* No one set of materials is so inclusive and useful that it can be used without regard to the many other aids which are available on the market. The program should not be dominated by the use of machines or a particular series of books. The wise, qualified teacher makes use of many different techniques and aids in dealing with a group of pupils who typically represent a wide range of reading ability levels.

5. *Solicit the cooperation of the total school staff.* All teachers and administrators must be made a part of the total planning of any new reading activity or facility which is to be established. Reading specialists must not be made to work in a vacuum.

6. *Plan for both periodic and continuous evaluation of the reading program or facility.* The use of standardized and informal devices as well as careful observation should be employed to assess the amount of reading growth experienced by the pupils. Open-end questionnaires should be completed by all teachers involved in any new endeavor and appropriate changes should be made in light of the predominant feelings which appear to prevail. Many programs are designed to alter

teacher attitudes, and the use of such questionnaires would give some indication relative to the degree of such changes.

7. *Explain the nature of new endeavors carefully to the parents.* If parents understand what kind of project is being undertaken, one can expect a much higher level of support from them. Since one of the leading purposes of programs is that of instituting some new innovation, parent support and understanding is imperative.

The preceding guidelines should be carefully considered before a proposal is constructed. Haphazard planning of a program can result in much wasted time and can, in some cases, result in more harm than good.

PROJECTED ROLE OF THE FEDERAL GOVERNMENT IN FUTURE ELEMENTARY READING PROGRAMS

No one person can predict the exact role of the Federal government with respect to future reading programs; however, on the basis of past and present trends, there is every reason to believe that funds will be available for innovative programs in reading and all other areas of education for an indefinite period. More cooperation among school districts and state departments of education will be solicited in order to prevent widespread duplication of effort.

Educators should never stop promoting sincere efforts to devise methods and materials which will help children to cope with the complex act of learning to read. Information concerning profitable endeavors should be shared among various educational agencies in order that legitimate research findings can be put to better use.

New efforts will no doubt be undertaken to help the culturally disadvantaged learn to read at higher levels of proficiency. Many of these projects will be underwritten by both Federal and private grants. More involvement by teachers of middle-class children will be encouraged.

Summary

Every teacher can be of much help in planning new reading programs. This author trusts that the information included in this chapter will help each reader to see his or her role in these endeavors.

Selected References

1. Heilman, Arthur W. *Principles and Practices of Teaching Reading.* Columbus, Ohio: Charles E. Merrill Books, 1967. Chapter 17.
2. Robinson, H. Alan and Rauch, Sidney J. *Guiding the Reading Program: A Reading Consultant's Handbook.* Chicago: Science Research Associates Inc., 1965. Resources Section.

3. Wilson, Robert M. *Diagnostic and Remedial Reading for Classroom and Clinic*. Columbus, Ohio: Charles E. Merrill Books, 1967. Chapter 11.

APPENDIX A

Book Clubs for Children and Youth

Advanced Readers' Program
   Grolier Enterprises Inc., 845 Third Ave., New York, New York 10022
   Advanced primary and early intermediate. Offers one book a month; minimum order four books a year.
All Girls Book Club
   155 North Wacker Drive, Chicago, Illinois 60606
American Education Publications
   55 High Street, Middletown, Connecticut 06457
   Offers book clubs for junior and senior high students in English, sciences, and social studies.
Beginning Readers' Program
   Grolier Enterprises Inc., 845 Third Ave., New York, New York 10022
   Preschool through primary grades. Offers one book a month; minimum order four books a year.
Best-in-Children's Books
   Nelson Doubleday, Inc., Garden City, New York 11531
   Offers books suitable for children ages 5–10.
Best Loved Girls' Books
   Nelson Doubleday, Inc., Garden City, New York 11531
   Offers books suitable for girls ages 11–15.
The Bookplan
   921 Washington Ave., Brooklyn, New York 11225
   Personalized service which chooses books for enrolled children and young people ages 8 mos. to 18 years through their histories and descriptions kept on file.
Calling All Girls Book Club
   Parents' Magazine Enterprises, 52 Vanderbilt Ave., New York, New York 10017
   Offers one book a month for girls ages 8–12; minimum order four books a year.
Parents' Magazine Book Club for Children
   Parents' Magazine Enterprises, Inc., Bergenfield, New Jersey 07621
   Offers a monthly book plan suitable for children ages 7–12.
Parents' Magazine's Read Aloud and Easy Reading Program
   52 Vanderbilt Ave., New York, New York 10017
   Offers books suitable for boys and girls ages 3–8.
Scholastic Book Services
   50 West 44th Street, New York, New York 10036
   Offers a wide selection of interest and ability books five times a year. Selection on a voluntary basis. Most books 25¢ or 35¢. Includes a dividend

book for every four or five books purchased.
See-saw Book Program grades K–1
Lucky Book Club grades 2–3
Arrow Book Club grades 4–6
Teen Age Book Club grades 7–9
Campus Book Club grades 10–12
Weekly Reader Children's Book Club
American Education Publications, 55 High Street, Middletown, Connecticut 06457
Offers five books a year in September, October, December, March, and May. Includes a dividend plan. Suitable for children ages 8–12.
Young Adults' Division of the Literary Guild
277 Park Avenue, New York, New York 10017
Young America Book Club
American Education Publications, 55 High Street, Middletown, Connecticut 06457
Young Folk's Book Club
1376 Coney Island Ave., Brooklyn, New York 11230
(Schools only)
Young People's Book Club
226 North Cass Ave., Westmont, Illinois 60559
Offers a book program suitable for children ages 8–13.

Further information concerning children's book clubs may be obtained from the following sources:

Children's Book Council
175 Fifth Avenue
New York, New York 10010

American Library Association
50 East Huron Street
Chicago, Illinois 60611

Children's Book Center
University of Chicago
Graduate Library School
Chicago, Illinois 60637

Irvin Hass
Book Club Consultants
65 Diana's Trail
Roslyn Estates, New York 11576

APPENDIX B

Periodicals for Children and Youth

American Childhood
American Childhood Magazine, 74 Park Avenue, Springfield, Mass.

American Education Publications
Education Center, Columbus, Ohio 43216
Our Times (Sr. H. S.) Weekly
Every Week (Sr. H. S.) Weekly
Current Events (Jr. H. S.) Weekly
Read Magazine (Jr. H. S.) Bi-weekly
Current Science (Jr. H. S.) Weekly
Science & Math Weekly (Sr. H. S.) Weekly
My Weekly Reader (K–6) Weekly

American Girl
Girl Scouts, Inc., 830 Third Avenue, New York, New York 10022
(10–16) Monthly

American Jr. Red Cross News
American National Red Cross, Washington, D.C. Free to schools with Red
Cross Donations. (7–14) Monthly.

Boys Life
Boy Scouts of America, 2 Park Avenue, New York, New York 10016
Boys, (10–18) Monthly.

Calling All Girls
Parents' Magazine Enterprises, Inc., Bergenfield, New Jersey 07621

Child Life
Clayton H. Ernest, 136 Federal Street, Boston, Mass. 02110

Children's Digest
Parents' Magazine Enterprises, Inc., Bergenfield, New Jersey 07621

Children's Playmate
A. R. Mueller Co., 3025 East 75th Street, Cleveland, Ohio 44105
(4–12) Monthly.

Civic Education Service
1733 K Street, N.W., Washington, D.C.
American Observer   32 Issues during school year.
Weekly News Review   32 Issues
Junior Review   32 Issues
Civic Leader   30 Issues

Flying
Ziff-Davis Publishing Co., 185 N. W. Avenue, Chicago, Illinois
(10–18) Monthly.

Geographic News Bulletin
National Geographic Society, 1146 16th Street, Washington, D.C. 20006
(7–12) Weekly.

Golden Magazine
Golden Press, North Road, Poughkeepsie, New York 12601
(7–12) Monthly.

Highlights
Highlights for Children, Inc., 2300 West Fifth Street, Columbus, Ohio 43216
(2–12) Monthly during school year.

Humpty Dumpty
Parents' Magazine Enterprises, Inc., Bergenfield, New Jersey 07621
(3–7) Monthly.

Jack and Jill
  Curtis Publishing Co., Independence Square, Philadelphia, Pennsylvania 19105
  (4–12) Monthly.
Junior Natural History
  American Museum of Natural History, Central Park West and 79th Street, New York, New York 10024
  (10–14) Monthly.
Model Airplane News
  Air Age, Inc., 551 Fifth Avenue, New York, New York 10010
  (7–16) Monthly.
National Geographic
  National Geographic Society, 1146 16th Street, Washington, D.C. 20006
  (12–up) Monthly.
Nature and Science
  American Museum of Natural History, Central Park West at 79th Street, New York, New York 10024
  (9–14) 17 issues.
Nature Magazine
  American Nature Association, 1214 16th Street, N.W., Washington, D.C. 20006
  (12–up) Monthly.
Plays: The Drama Magazine for Young People
  8 Arlington Street, Boston, Mass. 02116
  8 issues.
Popular Mechanics
  Popular Mechanics, 200 E. Ontario Street, Chicago, Illinois 60611
  (12–up) Monthly.
Popular Science
  Popular Science Publication Co., 353 Fourth Avenue, New York, New York 10010
  (12–up) Monthly.
Scholastic Magazines
  50 West 44th Street, New York, New York 10036
  Weekly during school year except where noted.

Senior Scholastic	(14–up)
World Week	(12–17)
Practical English	(13–up)
Scope	(12–17)
Junior Scholastic	(10–14)
Co-Ed	(12–up) Monthly
Literary Cavalcade	(14–up) Monthly
Senior Science	(13–up)
Science World	(11–16)
Newstime	(9–13)
News Explorer	(8–12)
News Trails	(7–10)
News Ranger	(6–9)

News Pilot   (6–7)
Young Citizen
Let's Find Out   Monthly
Summer Time   8 issues during summer
Vacation Fun   8 issues during summer
Merry-go-Round   8 issues during summer
Foreign language magazines also

School Arts Magazine
Davis Press, Inc., 44 Portland Street, Worcester, Mass.
(12–up) Monthly.

Story Parade
Story Parade Inc., 200 Fifth Avenue, New York, New York 10010
(7–12) Monthly.

Young American
Eton Publishing Corp., 32 East 57th Street, New York, New York
(12–18) Weekly during school year.

Young Wings
Junior Literary Guild, 9 Rockefeller Plaza, New York, New York 10020
(9–15) Free to subscribers of the Guild; separately, a fee is charged.
Monthly during school year.

APPENDIX C

Annotated Professional Book List for Teachers

This list has been carefully selected from the large array of books which have been published since 1963. No attempt has been made to curtail the number of books listed; therefore, each reader will need to select those books which meet his or her needs and financial resources. The annotations are designed to be a guide relative to the major aspects of a given book and not as a critique of that book.

1. Anderson, Verna D., Paul S. Anderson, Francis Ballantine, and Virgil M. Howes. *Readings in the Language Arts* (Second Edition). New York: The Macmillan Company, 1968.
   This is a concise paperback edition which contains important articles in all language arts areas. A series of discussions concerning the implications, applications, and analysis of linguistics is an important aspect of the new edition.

2. Barbe, Walter B. *Teaching Reading: Selected Materials*. New York: Oxford University Press, 1965.
   All important phases of reading instruction are discussed by the authors of the fifty-three articles in the volume. A unique feature is the inclusion of entire chapters from selected books. The paperback edition is broadly based since there are sections which are of interest to elementary, junior high, and senior high teachers.

3. Bond, Guy L. and Miles Tinker. *Reading Difficulties: Their Diagnosis and*

Correction (Second Edition). New York: Appleton-Century-Crofts, 1967.

The aim of the book is to give significant help to the classroom teacher, clinician, and remedial reading teacher in the diagnosis and correction of reading disabilities. A systematic and thorough presentation of the causes and treatment of all of the major disability areas is featured in the volume.

4. Bond, Guy L. and Eva Bond Wagner. *Teaching the Child to Read* (Fourth Edition). New York: The Macmillan Company, 1966.

This book is a basic methods source which includes practical teaching suggestions in all areas of reading. The philosophical structure of the book is based on research and the basic principles of child growth and development.

5. Chall, Jeanne. *Learning to Read: The Great Debate*. New York: The McGraw-Hill Book Company, 1967.

The findings of a three year study conducted under a grant from the Carnegie Corporation are reported by the author. Frank appraisals of currently used basal materials are made along with discussions concerning the importance of the code emphasis approach. The book has been reviewed in several journals.

6. Cordts, Anna D. *Phonics for the Reading Teacher*. New York: Holt, Rinehart and Winston, 1965.

Chapters on such topics as phonetics and phonics, the consonants in relation to phonics, and the syllabication of words are included. A unique aspect is the inclusion of informal tests at the close of each chapter.

7. Dawson, Mildred and Henry Bamman. *Fundamentals of Basic Reading Instruction* (Second Edition). New York: David McKay Company, Inc., 1963.

This book is designed primarily for the beginning teacher. Appropriate chapters on such topics as reading readiness, word-attack skills, oral reading, and comprehension provide valuable insights into the reading process.

8. DeBoer, John and Martha Dallman. *The Teaching of Reading* (Revised Edition). New York: Holt, Rinehart and Winston, Inc., 1964.

Theory and practice in each of the basic areas of reading are discussed in a meaningful manner. There are many specific teaching suggestions for developing skill in such areas as word recognition, comprehension, and oral reading.

9. Dechant, Emerald. *Improving the Teaching of Reading*. Englewood Cliffs, N.J.: Prentice-Hall, Inc., 1964.

The fifteen chapters of this book contain a wealth of provocative material of both a theoretical and practical nature for giving children adequate training in each of the basic facets of reading. The many illustrations help to emphasize the concepts. The book is extensively documented and includes many references.

10. Dechant, Emerald. *Diagnosis and Remediation of Reading Disability*. West Nyack, New York: Parker Publishing Co., Inc., 1968.

This volume is one of the most valuable books available for the reading teacher. Every aspect of remedial teaching is discussed in an authoritative manner.

11. De Hirsch, Katrina, Jeanette Jansky, and William S. Langford. *Predicting Reading Failure*. New York: Harper and Row, Publishers, 1966.

A report of the findings and implications of a major research study which was supported by the Health Research Council of New York is included in the volume. The material has much significance for those who are especially interested in the causes of reading failure.

12. Durr, William K. (Editor). *Reading Instruction: Dimensions and Issues*. Boston: Houghton Mifflin and Company, 1967.

The author has made a careful selection of outstanding articles which have been published since 1960. All major areas of reading are represented by writers who take differing viewpoints on instruction in reading in order to give the reader a broad base from which to reach conclusions regarding philosophy.

13. Figural, J. Allen (Editor). *IRA Conference Proceedings*. Newark, Delaware: International Reading Association, annually.

Each year the International Reading Association publishes the collection of addresses given at the annual IRA convention. The articles are valuable because of the frequent publication of professional opinion and research on many reading topics.

14. Fries, Charles. *Linguistics and Reading*. New York: Holt, Rinehart and Winston, Inc., 1963.

One of the objectives of this book has been the attempt to bring together a non-technical descriptive survey of current linguistic knowledge. Other information is related to the structure of the reading process in light of linguistics. Materials and methods involved in the linguistic approach are described.

15. Gans, Roma. *Fact and Fiction About Phonics*. New York: The Bobbs-Merrill Company, Inc., 1964.

Dr. Gans describes the popular misconceptions about teaching phonics and delineates the proper procedures which should be employed in making phonics instruction useful to children. Helpful references for wider reading are included in the paperback volume.

16. Gans, Roma. *Common Sense in Teaching Reading*. New York: Bobbs-Merrill Company, Inc., 1963.

This volume is addressed to both parents and teachers since it is the author's contention that only through cooperative efforts of both home and school can one expect a full understanding of the value of reading in the life of a child. Practical examples of learning situations are described.

17. Harris, Albert J. (Editor). *Readings on Reading Instruction*. New York: David McKay Company, Inc., 1963.

The ninety-nine readings selected by the editor represent a balanced collection of articles in every major phase of reading instruction. Careful attention has been given to the use of selections which have been authored by writers who have made significant contributions to reading education since 1941.

18. Heilman, Arthur W. *Phonics in Proper Perspective.* Columbus, Ohio: Charles E. Merrill Books, Inc., 1964.

Purposes, limitations, and practices involved in phonics instruction which should be understood by every teacher are described in this small volume. The rationale which underlies particular instructional practices is explained.

19. Heilman, Arthur W. *Principles and Practices of Teaching Reading* (Second Edition). Columbus, Ohio: Charles E. Merrill Books, Inc., 1967.

The new edition of this familiar methods book contains chapters on beginning reading, linguistics, individualized reading, study skills, and related topics. Summary statements are placed at the close of each chapter to stimulate and challenge the thinking of each reader.

20. Jennings, Frank G. *This Is Reading.* New York: Bureau of Publications, Teachers College, Columbia University, 1965.

Mr. Jennings assumes the position that the formation of worthwhile reading attitudes and skills is a multi-faceted responsibility of the family, community, and the school; therefore teachers, parents, and lay adults in general will find the volume stimulating and challenging.

21. King, Martha L., Bernice D. Ellinger, and Willavene Wolf (Editors). *Critical Reading.* New York: J. B. Lippincott Company, 1967.

The editors have selected fifty pertinent articles on critical reading on such topics as the importance and nature of critical reading, critical reading in relation to other kinds of thinking and creative behavior, teaching critical reading, and research in critical reading. This is one of the few volumes devoted exclusively to this topic.

22. Lamb, Pose. *Linguistics in Proper Perspective.* Columbus, Ohio: Charles E. Merrill Publishing Company, 1967.

Lamb's book provides the pre-service and in-service teacher with a well-organized yet concise description of the relationship of linguistics to the teaching of the total language arts area. The glossary of terms relating to the study of linguistics is included in order to help the reader grasp a fuller understanding of the major concepts involved in this important field.

23. Larrick, Nancy and John A. Stoops (Editors). *What Is Reading Doing to the Child?* Danville, Illinois: The Interstate Printers and Publishers, Inc., 1967.

This paperback edition is a compilation of papers which were given at the 1967 Lehigh Reading Conference. Theory, practice, and words of reform are treated in the volume of slightly over one-hundred pages. The reactions of pupils to various reading questions are included.

24. MacCampbell, James C. *Readings in the Language Arts in the Elementary School.* Boston: D. C. Heath and Company, 1964.

This book brings together a large number of carefully selected articles and essays which are concerned with the major aspects of instruction in the language arts at the elementary school level.

25. Mazurkiewicz, Albert J. *New Perspectives in Reading Instruction.* New York: Pitman Publishing Corporation, 1964.

This collection of speeches and papers from the Lehigh University Conferences as well as from other sources encompasses all of the important areas of reading instruction, such as the nature of reading, reading in the content areas, and the analysis of the different approaches to reading.

26. McKee, Paul. *Reading: A Program of Instruction for the Elementary School*. Boston: Houghton Mifflin Company, 1966.

    The author has composed an extensive, detailed description and explanation of what he feels is a carefully built program of reading instruction for elementary pupils. The material is presented in a sequential nature and is authoritative from the standpoint of research and the long experience of the writer as a reading professional.

27. McKim, Margaret and Helen Caskey. *Guiding Growth in Reading* (Second Edition). New York: The Macmillan Company, 1963.

    The authors have included many activities which the classroom teacher might use in day-to-day reading instruction. The book is not intended to be prescriptive, since the writers take the position that each teacher must be creative in adapting teaching techniques to fit the needs of individual pupils. Extensive selections on both developmental and remedial reading are provided.

28. Otto, Wayne and Richard McMenemy. *Corrective and Remedial Teaching*. Boston: Houghton Mifflin Company, 1966.

    The major phases of diagnosis and remediation of reading, spelling, arithmetic, and handwriting are discussed. Lists of specific tests, materials, and teaching suggestions constitute a significant aspect of the total presentation.

29. Robinson, H. Alan and Sidney J. Rauch. *Guiding the Reading Program*. Chicago: Science Research Associates, Inc., 1965.

    This work brings together a series of operational guidelines which should be helpful to a reading consultant in the administration of his duties. The appendix contains information relative to books and materials for teachers of reading, books and materials for the reading consultant, books and materials for parents, and the names and addresses of educational publishers.

30. Schell, Leo M. and Paul C. Burns (Editors). *Remedial Reading: an Anthology of Sources*. Boston: Allyn and Bacon, Inc., 1968.

    This compilation consists of fifty-five selected articles in such areas as causal and associated factors; identification, diagnosis, prognosis; principles of instruction; instructional procedures; readers with emotional problems; instructional materials; and organizing and administering a remedial reading program.

31. Schubert, Delwyn G. and Theodore L. Torgerson (Editors). *Readings in Reading*. New York: Thomas Y. Crowell Company, 1968.

    The authors have included over eighty selected readings to lend the reader insight into such aspects as theory, research, and past and present practices in reading instruction.

32. Sleisenger, Lenore. *Guidebook for the Volunteer Reading Teacher*. New York: Teachers College Press, Columbia University, 1965.

    This volume is one of the few works devoted to this particular topic. Information relating to methods and materials, appropriate books for remedial reading, and evaluation and referral are included.

33. Smith, Nila B. *American Reading Instruction*. Newark, Delaware: International Reading Association, 1965.

Dr. Smith's first edition of this title appeared in 1934. The author has very carefully described the major historical movements in reading instruction since America became a nation. Every student of reading will find the volume both stimulating and fascinating.

34. Smith, Nila B. *Reading Instruction for Today's Children*. Englewood Cliffs, N.J.: Prentice-Hall, Inc., 1963.

The acquaintance of both students and teachers with all aspects of current reading theory and pertinent research in reading, as well as the application of this theory and research to actual teaching of pupils in the classroom, are the two major objectives of this volume. Many teaching suggestions are outlined for each of the major reading skill areas.

35. Strang, Ruth. *Diagnostic Teaching of Reading*. New York: McGraw-Hill Book Company, 1964.

The author of this work takes the position that the diagnosis of reading difficulties is never an end in itself and should be an intrinsic part of teaching. Appropriate sections are provided for discussions concerning group procedures and individual methods.

36. Tinker, Miles A. *Bases for Effective Reading*. Minneapolis: University of Minnesota Press, 1965.

A summary of the results and conclusions of significant research conducted by the writer concerning the physiological aspects of the reading process and the factors which are correlated with reading problems and difficulties are included in this well-documented volume. One of the sections deals with the much discussed role of eye movements in effective reading development.

37. Wilson, Robert M. *Diagnostic and Remedial Reading*. Columbus, Ohio: Charles E. Merrill Books, Inc., 1967.

The role and relationship of the classroom teacher and the reading clinician are discussed in the areas of diagnosis and remediation. Unique to books in this area is a chapter devoted to the parents' role in diagnosis, remediation and prevention. Many practical suggestions for aiding pupils in different reading problem areas are carefully outlined in the volume.

38. Witty, Paul A., Alma Moore Freeland, and Edith H. Grotberg. *The Teaching of Reading*. Boston: D. C. Heath and Company, 1966.

The authors have compiled the book from the developmental point of view and have covered every major aspect of reading instruction. The results of the long study and research by the senior author are interwoven appropriately with the various topics. The philosophy that reading is sequential and extends from the elementary school into adult life is promoted.

39. Zintz, Miles V. *Corrective Reading*. Dubuque, Iowa: Wm. C. Brown Company, Inc., 1966.

Various segments of remedial reading instruction are dealt with in light of the author's wide experience as a teacher and professor. Many activities are described which should be of use to the classroom teacher. Illustrations of materials are included.

APPENDIX D

Professional Journal List for Teachers

The following list constitutes a portion of the professional journals which contain articles in reading instruction. Due to frequent change in subscription price, no attempt has been made to include this information.

Academic Therapy Quarterly (four times a year) Academic Therapy Publications, 1543 Fifth Street, San Rafael, California 94901

Education (September–May) Bobbs-Merrill Company, 4300 West 62nd Street, Indianapolis, Indiana 46286

Elementary English (October–May) National Council of Teachers of English, 508 South Sixth Street, Champaign, Illinois 61822

Elementary School Journal (October–May) University of Chicago Press, 5750 Ellis Avenue, Chicago, Illinois 60637

Grade Teacher (September–May) Teachers Publishing Corporation, Darien, Connecticut 07820

Instructor (10 issues a year) F. A. Owen Publishing Company, 5 Bank Street, Danville, New York 14437

Journal of Learning Disabilities (Monthly) The Professional Press Publishers, Room 1410, Five North Wabash Avenue, Chicago, Illinois 60602

Journal of Reading (6 times a year) International Reading Association, Box 695, Newark, Delaware 19711

Journal of Reading Specialist (4 issues a year) Dr. A. J. Mazurkiewicz, Reading Laboratory, Rochester Institute of Technology, Rochester, New York 14608

N.E.A. Journal (September–May) National Educational Association of the United States, 1201 16th Street, N.W., Washington, D.C. 20036

Reading Horizons (Quarterly) Dorothy J. McGinnis, Director, Psycho-Educational Clinic, Western Michigan University, Kalamazoo, Michigan

Reading Research Quarterly (4 times a year) International Reading Association, Box 695, Newark, Delaware 19711

Reading Teacher (8 times a year) International Reading Association, Box 695, Newark, Delaware 19711

The Journal of Reading Behavior (4 times a year beginning January, 1969) Journal of Reading Behavior, College of Education, University of Georgia, Athens, Georgia 30601

The Reading Newsreport (7 issues a year) The Reading Newsreport, P. O. Box 8036, Washington, D.C. 20024

APPENDIX E

Instructional Materials

A variety of materials prepared by publishers can be used in assisting pupils to improve their reading. The reading level at which these materials are appropriate is indicated; pupils above this level can often use these materials with profit to correct specific difficulties. Appreciation is extended to Dr. Donavon Lumpkin, Director of the Reading Center, Ball State University, who compiled the information in Appendixes E, F, and G and who gave us permission to print it in this volume. Space limitations prevented the listing of all materials available from publishers.

AMERICAN EDUCATION PUBLICATIONS, Education Center, Columbus, Ohio 43216

Weekly Reader Practice Books	
Phonics and Word Power Programs 1–3	First–Third
Science Reading Skills	K–Sixth
Readiness for Map Skills	Primary
Map Reading Skills, 4 and 6	Intermediate
Read–Study–Think 2–6	Second–Sixth
Independent Activities	
Unit Books	First–Second
Creative Expression Series	
Imagine and Write 3 and 4	Third–Fourth
English	
Diagnose and Improve Your English Skills	Sixth–Ninth
10 Plays and Choral Readings	Seventh–Ninth
Stories You Can Finish	Seventh–Ninth
Discovery Series	
Zip's Book of Wheels	Kindergarten
Zip's Book of Animals	Kindergarten
Zip's Book of Puzzles	Kindergarten

BARNELL LOFT, LTD., 111 South Centre Avenue, Rockville Centre, New York 11571

Working With Sounds	
Books A–D	First–Fourth
Using The Context	
Books A–F	First–Sixth
Locating The Answer	
Books B–D	Second–Fourth
Following Directions	
Books A–D	First–Fourth
Getting The Facts	
Books A–F	Third–Fifth
Getting The Main Idea	
Book A	First

Drawing Conclusions
    Book A   First

CALIFORNIA TEST BUREAU, Del Monte Research Park, Monterey, California 93940

Lessons for Self-Instruction in Basic Skills
    Mechanics of English Series CD   Fifth-Sixth
        Sentence Patterns
        Verbs, Modifiers, and Pronouns
        Capitalization
        Punctuation
    Reading Comprehension Series ED   Fifth-Sixth
        Reference Skills
        Read To Understand—Interpretations I
        Know What You Read—Interpretations II
        Following Directions
        Reading Interpretations (Series EF)   Seventh–Eighth

CONTINENTAL PRESS, INC., Elizabethtown, Pennsylvania 17022

Reading Readiness Series, Reading Fundamentals Program
    Rhyming Books, Levels 1 and 2   K–First
    Visual Motor Skills, Levels 1 and 2   K–First
    Visual Discrimination, Levels 1 and 2   K–First
    Beginning Sounds, Levels 1 and 2   K–First
    Independent Activities, Levels 1 and 2   K–First

Reading-Thinking Skills
    Primer Level—Grade 6   Primer–Sixth
    (Two Workbooks for each grade level)

EDUCATIONAL DEVELOPMENTAL LABORATORIES, Huntington, New York 11746

Science
    Boxes C–I   Third–Ninth

Social Science
    Boxes CC–II   Third–Ninth

Reference Skills
    Boxes OOO–III   Third–Ninth

FOLLETT PUBLISHING COMPANY, 1010 West Washington Blvd., Chicago, Illinois 60607

Sounds We Use Book 1   First

GARRARD PRESS, Champaign, Illinois 61820

Readiness for Reading	Primary

Happy Bears Reading Set	Pre-Primer
My Puzzle Books 1 and 2	Primary

GINN AND COMPANY, 450 W. Algonquin Road, Arlington Heights, Illinois 60005

Sounds We Use	
Set 1—Consonant Sounds (8 filmstrips & manual)	Primary
Set 2—Vowel Sounds (4 filmstrips & manual)	Primary

Creative Thinking Materials	
Ideabooks	
Can You Imagine? (Teacher's Guide)	First–Third
Invitations To Thinking and Doing (Teachers Guide)	Fourth–Sixth
Invitations To Speaking and Writing Creatively	
(Teachers Guide)	Sixth–Eighth

Ginn Vocabulary Program	Seventh–Ninth

GROLIER EDUCATIONAL CORPORATION, Dept. RA–7, 845 Third Avenue, New York, New York 10022

Reading Attainment System	Seventh–Twelfth

HARCOURT, BRACE & WORLD, INC., 7555 Caldwell Avenue, Chicago, Illinois 60648

Speech-To-Print Phonics (Teacher's Manual)	Primary

Language For Daily Use (Teacher's Manual)	Fourth–Sixth

D. C. HEATH AND COMPANY, 1815 Prairie Avenue, Chicago, Illinois 60616

English Is Our Language, Levels 4, 5, 6	
Teacher's Guide and Key	Fourth–Sixth

It's Fun To Find Out	
The Fireman and six other titles	First

HUBBARD COMPANY, P.O. Drawer 100, Defiance, Ohio 43512

My Reading Design Form A	Third–Fourth
My Reading Design Form B	Fifth–Sixth

LAIDLAW BROTHERS (Doubleday & Company) Thatcher & Madison, River Forest, Illinois 60305

Study Exercises for Developing Reading Skills Series	
Books A–C	Fourth–Sixth

LYONS AND CARNAHAN, 407 East 25th Street, Chicago, Illinois 60616

My Word Book Series	
Workbook	First
Books 2–8 plus workbook (Teacher's Edition)	Second–Eighth

Phonics We Use	
Books A–G (Teacher's Edition)	Primer-Sixth
Learning Games Kit (Ten games in a series)	Primer-Sixth

THE MACMILLAN COMPANY, 434 South Wabash Avenue, Chicago, Illinois 60605

Reading Spectrum—Spectrum of Skills	
Word Analysis	First–Fifth
Vocabulary Development	First–Sixth
Reading Comprehension	First–Sixth
Teacher's Guide for Spectrum of Skills	

McCORMICK-MATHERS PUBLISHING COMPANY, Box 2212, 1400 East English Street, Wichita, Kansas 67201

Building Reading Skills (Teacher's Guide & Phonics Skill Builders)	
Speedboat Book	Second
Streamliner Book	Second
Jet Plane	Third
Rocket Book	Fourth
Atomic Submarine	Fifth
Space Ship Book	Sixth

Puzzle Workbooks (Four Workbooks)	Readiness–
	Second

CHARLES E. MERRILL BOOKS, 1300 Alum Creek Drive, Columbus, **Ohio** 43216

Diagnostic Reading Workbooks	
Adventure Trails	Fourth
Exploring Today	Fifth
Looking Ahead	Sixth

New Phonics Skilltext Series	
Going Places in Readiness	Readiness
My Alphabet Book	Primer–First
Workbooks, A–D	First–Fourth

Reading Adventures	
Book C	Fifth–Sixth

Reading Skilltext Series	
Bibs	First
Nicky	Second
Uncle Funny Bunny	Third
Uncle Ben	Fourth
Tom Trott	Fifth
Pat, The Pilot	Sixth
Teacher's Editions for all of previous titles	

MODERN CURRICULUM PRESS, P.O. Box 9, Berea, Ohio 44017

Phonics Is Fun Books 1 and 2 (Teacher's Manual and Workbook available)	First–Second

READERS DIGEST SERVICES, INC., Educational Division, Pleasantville, New York 10570

New Reading Skill Builders (1967)	
Levels 1–4, Parts 1, 2 (Teacher's Ed. and Practice Pads)	First–Fourth

Reading Skill Builders (1960)	
Level 1, Parts A, B, 1, 2	First
Levels 2–6, Parts 1, 2, 3 and Teacher's Ed.	Second–Sixth

Growth In Word Power

SCIENCE RESEARCH ASSOCIATES, 259 East Erie Street, Chicago, Illinois 60611

SRA Reading Laboratories	Reading Levels	For Use In:
Lab I (Word Games)	1.3 to 3.0	Primary
Lab Ia	1.2 to 3.0	First
Lab Ib	1.4 to 4.0	Second
Lab Ic	1.4 to 5.0	Third
Elementary Edition	2.0 to 9.0	Elementary
Lab IIa	2.0 to 7.0	Fourth
Lab IIb	3.0 to 8.0	Fifth
Lab IIc	4.0 to 9.0	Sixth
Lab IIIa 1957 and 1962	3.0 to 12.0	Jr. High

Lab IIIb	5.0 to 12.0	Eighth-Ninth
Lab IVa	8.0 to 14.0	High School

Pilot Libraries		
IIa	2.0 to 7.0	Fourth
IIc	4.0 to 9.0	Sixth
IIIb	6.0 to 11.0	Eighth-Ninth

Reading For Understanding	
Junior Edition	Third–Eighth
General Edition	Fifth–Twelfth

Study Skills	
Graph and Picture Study Skills	Fourth–Sixth
Organizing and Reporting Skills	Fourth–Sixth
Map and Globe Skills	Fourth–Sixth

Spelling Word Laboratory	
IIb	Fifth

L. W. SINGER COMPANY, INC., 5601 Northwest Highway, Chicago, Illinois 60646

Structural Reading Series	
Teacher's Kit	First
A—We Learn To Listen	Readiness
B—Picture Dictionary	Readiness
C—We Discover Reading	First
D—We Read and Write	First
E—We Read More and More	Second
F—Now We Read Everything	Second

STECK-VAUGHN COMPANY, Box 2028, Austin, Texas 78767

Reading Essentials Series	
(Six Titles with Teacher's Manuals)	First–Sixth

TEACHERS COLLEGE PRESS, 525 West 120th Street, New York, New York 10027

Gates-Peardon Practice Exercises in Reading	
Book III, Type A, B, C, D (manual)	Third
Book IV, Type A, B, C, D (manual)	Fourth
Book V, Type A, B, C, D (manual)	Fifth
Book VI, Type A, B, C, D (manual)	Sixth

Gates-Peardon Reading Exercises	First–Eighth
McCall-Crabbs Standard Test Lessons in Reading	
Books A–E (manual)	Third–Seventh

Read Along With Me Series	
Teacher's Manual	Primer

TEACHING RESOURCES, 100 Boylston Street, Boston, Massachusetts 02116

Visual-Motor Perception Teaching Materials
Perceptual Motor-Development
Sequential Perceptual-Motor Exercises
Directional-Spatial-Pattern Board Exercises
Eye-Hand Coordination Exercises
Perceptual-Motor Teaching Materials

WEBSTER DIVISION, McGraw-Hill Book Company, Manchester Road, Manchester, Missouri 63011

Classroom Reading Clinic	Elementary
Webster Word Wheels	Third–Sixth
Conquests in Reading (Teacher's Edition)	Elementary
The Magic World of Dr. Spello (Teacher's Edition)	Elementary

Practice Readers	
Books 1–4	Third–Sixth
Basic Goals in Reading	Second–Fourth
New Practice Readers	
Books A–G (Answer Keys Available)	Second–Eighth

XEROX CURRICULUM PROGRAMS, Dept. C, Xerox Corporation, 600 Madison Avenue, New York, New York 10022

Words in Color	
Teacher's Guide	Initial Teaching
Books 1, 2, 3	of Reading
Word Building Book	
Worksheets 1–14	
Charts	
Phonics Code Charts	
Wallcharts	

The Literature Sampler	
Junior Edition	Fourth–Sixth

APPENDIX F

High Interest, Low-Vocabulary Books

Following is a list of vocabulary-controlled books which might be used for independent reading. The reading levels have been estimated by such criteria as vocabulary level, vocabulary load, sentence length, picture clues, size of print, conceptual load, and experience using the book with children whose approximate reading levels are known. An "X" to the right of column 6 indicates that a given material is suitable for pupils at the junior or senior high levels.

ALLYN AND BACON, 310 W. Polk Street, Chicago, Illinois 60607

	R	PP	P	1	2	3	4	5	6
Adventures in Science with Judy and Joe			x						

AMERICAN BOOK COMPANY, 55 Fifth Avenue, New York 3, New York

	R	PP	P	1	2	3	4	5	6
American Reading Round Table Series									
Who Me? (five other titles)	x								
I Can (seven other titles)		x							
Pets and Places (Five other titles)			x						
Who Is It? (five other titles)				x					
A House for Mrs. Hopper (7 other titles)					x				
Sir Danny's Dragon (5 other titles)						x			

BENEFIC PRESS, 1900 North Narragansett, Chicago, Illinois 60639

	R	PP	P	1	2	3	4	5	6
Adventure Series									
Adventures Fishing						x			
Adventures Hunting							x		
Adventure Series									
On Days We Like	x								
On Winter Days	x								
On Days for Fun		x							
As We Go			x						
On Our Way				x					
All Age Books									
Peter and the Unlucky Rocket					x				
Peter and the Big Balloon					x				
Peter and the Rocket Ship						x			
Peter and the Two Hour Moon						x			
Peter and the Moon Trip						x			
Butternut Bill Series									
Butternut Bill	x								
Butternut Bill and the Bee Tree	x								
Butternut Bill and the Big Catfish	x								
Butternut Bill and the Bear		x							
Butternut Bill and the Little River		x							
Butternut Bill and the Big Pumpkin		x							
Cowboy Sam and the Rodeo					x				
Cowboy Sam and the Airplane						x			
Cowboy Sam and the Indians (workbook)						x			
Cowboy Sam and the Rustlers						x			
Dan Frontier Series									
Dan Frontier	x								
Dan Frontier and the New House	x								

	R	PP	P	1	2	3	4	5	6
Dan Frontier Goes Hunting			x						
Dan Frontier and the Big Cat			x						
Dan Frontier, Trapper				x					
Dan Frontier and the Wagon Train					x				
Dan Frontier Scouts for the Army					x				
Dan Frontier, Sheriff						x			
Dan Frontier Goes Exploring						x			
Dan Frontier Goes to Congress							x		
Manual for Series									
Easy to Read Books									
Pretty Bird		x							
Invitation to Adventure Series									
On Days We Like		x							
On Winter Days		x							
On Days for Fun			x						
As We Go				x					
On Our Way					x				
Jerry Series									
Jerry		x							
Jerry Goes Riding			x						
Jerry Goes Fishing				x					
Jerry Goes on a Picnic					x				
Jerry Goes to the Circus						x			
Moonbeam Series									
Moonbeam Is Caught		x							
Moonbeam at the Rocket Port			x						
Moonbeam and the Rocket Ride				x					
Moonbeam and Dan Starr				x					
Sailor Jack Series									
Sailor Jack		x							
Sailor Jack and the Jet Plane			x						
Sailor Jack's New Friend				x					
Sailor Jack and the Target Ship					x				
Sailor Jack Goes North						x			
Space Travel Books									
Peter and the Unlucky Rocket					x				
Peter and the Big Balloon					x				
Peter and the Rocket Ship						x			
Peter and the Two Hour Moon						x			
Peter and the Moon Trip						x			
Tom Logan Series									
Pony Rider		x							
Cattle Drive			x						
Tommy O'Toole Series									
Tommy O'Toole and Larry				x					
Tommy O'Toole at the Fair					x				
Tommy O'Toole and the Forest Fire						x			

	R	PP	P	1	2	3	4	5	6
World of Adventure Series									
Flight to the South Pole					x				
The Lost Uranium Mine					x				
Hunting Grizzly Bears						x			
Fire on the Mountain						x			
City Beneath the Sea							x		
The Search for Piranha								x	
Viking Treasure									x
Teacher's Guide for Series									
Activity Book for Series									

BOBBS-MERRILL CO., INC., 4300 West 62nd St., Indianapolis, Ind. 46206

	R	PP	P	1	2	3	4	5	6
Childhood of Famous Americans Series									
Clara Barton, Girl Nurse						x			
George Carver, Boy Scientist						x			
Amelia Earhart, Kansas Girl						x			
Abe Lincoln, Frontier Boy						x			
Babe Ruth, Baseball Boy						x			
(142 additional titles including						x			
famous men and women)									

CHILDREN'S PRESS, INC., Jackson Blvd. & Racine Ave., Chicago, Illinois 60607

	R	PP	P	1	2	3	4	5	6
Frontiers of America Series									
Hunters Blaze the Trails							x		
Log Fort Adventures							x		
Mail Riders							x		
Pioneers on Early Waterways							x		
Steamboats to the West							x		
Wagons Over the Mountains							x		
I Want to be Series									
I Want to be a Dentist					x				
I Want to be an Airplane Hostess					x				

DELL PUBLISHING CO., INC., 750 Third Avenue, New York, New York 10017

	R	PP	P	1	2	3	4	5	6
Yearling Books									
Elephl, The Cat with the High I.Q.					x	x	x	x	x
John F. Kennedy (And 8 other titles)					x	x	x	x	x

DOUBLEDAY AND CO., INC., Garden City, L.I., New York 11531

	R	PP	P	1	2	3	4	5	6
Signal Books									
Civil War Sailor							x		
Baseball Spark Plug							x		
Gracie							x		
Hi Packett Jumping Center							x		
Dirt Track Danger							x		
Green Light for Sandy							x		
Let's Go to the Brook				x	x	x			
Let's Go Outdoors				x	x	x			
Mary Jane							x	x	x

FIELD EDUCATIONAL PUBLICATIONS, INC., 609 Mission Street, San Francisco, Calif. 94105

	R	PP	P	1	2	3	4	5	6
Checkered Flag Series									
Wheels					x				
Riddler					x				
Bearcat					x				
Smashup					x				
Deep Sea Adventure									
The Sea Hunt					x				
Treasure Under the Sea					x				
Submarine Rescue					x				
The Pearl Divers						x			
Frogman in Action						x			
Danger Below						x			
Whale Hunt							x		
Rocket Divers							x		
Teacher's Manual									
Jim Forest Series									
Jim Forest and Ranger Don (Practice Bk)					x				
Jim Forest and the Bandits (Practice Bk)					x				
Jim Forest and the Mystery Hunter					x				
Jim Forest and Dead Man's Peak						x			
Jim Forest and the Flood						x			
Jim Forest and Lone Wolf Gulch						x			
Teacher's Manual									
Morgan Bay Mystery Series									
Mystery of Morgan Castle						x			
Mystery of the Marble Angel						x			
Mystery of the Musical Ghost						x			
Mystery of the Midnight Visitor							x		
Mystery of the Missing Marlin							x		
Mystery of Marks' Island							x		
The Mystery of the Myrmidon's Journey							x		
The Mystery of the Maraude's Gold							x		
Teacher's Manual for the Series									
Reading Motivated Series									
Desert Treasure							x		
The Mysterious Swamp Rider							x		
The Secret of Lonesome Valley							x		
The Time Machine Series									
(33⅓ r.p.m. record for each title)									
Leonard Visits Space	x								
Leonard Visits the Ocean Floor		x							
Leonard Discovers America			x						
Leonard Visits Dinosaur Land				x					
Teacher's Manual for Series									
Wildlife Adventure Series									
Gatie the Alligator							x		
Sleeky the Otter							x		

	R	PP	P	1	2	3	4	5	6
Skipper the Dolphin								x	
Tawny, the Mountain Lion								x	
Teacher's Manual for Series									

FOLLETT PUBLISHING CO., 1010 W. Washington Blvd., Chicago, Illinois 60607

	R	PP	P	1	2	3	4	5	6
Just Beginning-To-Read Series									
The Funny Baby		x							
The Three Bears		x							
The Three Goats		x							
The Three Little Pigs		x							
Toy Box Tales									
The Fish			x						
Beginning to Read Books									
Gertie the Duck				x					
My Own Little House				x					
Nobody Listens to Andrew				x					
Too Many Dogs				x					
Abraham Lincoln					x				
The Boy Who Would Not Say His Name					x				
Interesting Reading Series									
Buried Gold					x				
Mystery of Broken Wheel Ranch					x				
Adventures in Space						x			
First Adventure at Sea						x			
First Man in Space						x			
The Indian Fighters						x			
Mary Elizabeth and Mr. Lincoln						x			

GARRARD PRESS, 510 North Hickory Street, Champaign, Illinois 61820

	R	PP	P	1	2	3	4	5	6
Basic Vocabulary Series									
Animal Stories					x				
Bear Stories					x				
Circus Stories					x				
Dog Stories					x				
Elephant Stories					x				
Folk Stories					x				
Horse Stories					x				
Irish Stories					x				
Lion and Tiger Stories					x				
Lodge Stories					x				
Navaho Stories					x				
Pueblo Stories					x				
Tepee Stories					x				
Why Stories					x				
Wigwam Stories					x				
Discovery Books									
Daniel Boone					x				
Clara Barton					x				
George Washington Carver					x				

	R	PP	P	1	2	3	4	5	6
Benjamin Franklin					x				
Henry Hudson					x				
Lafayette					x				
Abraham Lincoln					x				
Theodore Roosevelt					x				
First Books									
Big, Bigger, Biggest				x					
Dog Pals				x					
I Like Cats				x					
In the Woods				x					
Monkey Friends				x					
On the Farm				x					
Some Are Small				x					
Tommy's Pets				x					
Zoo Is Home				x					
Folklore Books									
Stories from Alaska						x			
Stories from Hawaii						x			
Stories from Japan						x			
Junior Science Series									
Stars					x				
Pleasure Reading Series									
Andersen Stories						x			
Bible Stories						x			
Fairy Stories						x			
Famous Stories						x			
Far East Stories						x			
Gospel Stories						x			
Greek Stories						x			
Gulliver's Stories						x			
Old World Stories						x			
Robin Hood Stories						x			
Robinson Crusoe						x			
Reading Shelf									
The Farmer and the Witch				x					
John Henry, Steel-Drivin' Man						x			
Poetry For Holidays						x			
Indians									
Crazy Horse						x			
Scouting									
The Girl Scout Story						x			
Baden-Powell						x			
Holidays									
The Holiday Book EASTER						x			
Spring Holidays						x			
Sports									
Decathlon Men							x		
The Game of Baseball							x		

	R	PP	P	1	2	3	4	5	6
Baseball; Hall of Fame Stories of Champions							X		
The Game of Football							X		

GLOBE BOOK COMPANY, 175 Fifth Avenue, New York, New York 10010

	R	PP	P	1	2	3	4	5	6
Modern Literature Series									
The Bridges at Toko-Ri									X
Jack London's Call of the Wild									X
The Last Days of Pompeii									X
One Act Plays for Today									X
Stories for Teen-agers, Book I									X
Stories for Teen-agers, Book II									X
Stories for Today's Youth, Book I									X
Adapted Classics									
From Earth to Moon							X	X	
The Prince and the Pauper							X	X	
Twenty Thousand Leagues Under the Sea							X	X	
American Folklore and Legends (Guide)						X	X		
Myths and Folk Tales Around the World (Guide)						X	X		

GROSSET AND DUNLAP, INC., 51 Madison Avenue, New York, New York 10010

		R	PP	P	1	2	3	4	5	6
An Early-Start Preschool Reader	*Words in Vocabulary*									
The Sandwich	11									
The Pond	14									
The Tent	15									
The Rabbit	15									
Ann Likes Red	16									
Ballerina Bess	25									
Bill and the Fish	26									
On the Ranch	30									
One, Two	30									
Big Beds and Little Beds	33									
Jumping	34									
A Happy Day	39									
The Bus from Chicago	49									
Up and Down	50									
The Rabbit and the Turtle	66									
Poems	107									
Easy Reader Books										
Mr. Pine's Mixed-up Signs						X				
A Train for Tommy						X				
Signature Books										
Madame Curie										X
We Were There Books										
Lewis and Clark										X
Young Readers Bookshelf										
Animal Stories										
Daniel Boone										

	R	PP	P	1	2	3	4	5	6
GUILD PRESS, INC., Poughkeepsie, New York									
Adventure in Space Man-Made Satellites Space Pilots									

E. M. HALE AND COMPANY, 1201 S. Hastings Way, Eau Clair, Wisconsin 54702

	R	PP	P	1	2	3	4	5	6
All About Books									
All About Dinosaurs							x	x	x
All About Engines and Power							x	x	x
All About Our 50 States							x	x	x
All About the Symphony Orchestra							x	x	x
All About Undersea Exploration							x	x	x
Beginner Books									
Ann Can Fly				x	x				
Are You My Mother?				x	x				
A Big Ball of String				x	x				
The Big Jump and Other Stories				x	x				
The Big Honey Hunt				x	x				
Book of Laughs				x	x				
Book of Riddles				x	x				
The Cat in the Hat Comes Back				x	x				
Cowboy Andy				x	x				
A Fish Out of Water				x	x				
A Fly Went by				x	x				
Go, Dog, Go!				x	x				
Green Eggs and Ham				x	x				
I Was Kissed by a Seal at the Zoo				x	x				
The King's Wish				x	x				
Little Black, A Pony				x	x				
Look Out for Pirates!				x	x				
More Riddles				x	x				
One Fish Two Fish Red Fish Blue Fish				x	x				
Put Me in the Zoo				x	x				
Robert, The Rose Horse				x	x				
Sam and the Firefly				x	x				
Snow				x	x				
Stop That Ball				x	x				
Ten Apples Up on Top				x	x				
The Whales Go by				x	x				
You Will Go to the Moon				x	x				
Easy to Read Books									
Adventure at Black Rock Cave					x				
Champ, Gallant Collie					x				
Everything Happens to Stuey					x				
Found: One Orange-Brown Horse					x				
Katie and Sad Noise					x				
Mystery of the Musical Umbrella					x				
No Room for a Dog					x				

	R	PP	P	1	2	3	4	5	6
Old Rosie, the Horse Nobody Understood						x			
The Runaway Flea Circus						x			
The Snake That Went to School						x			
The Terrible Mr. Twitmeyer						x			
Why It's a Holiday						x			
Easy to Read Science Library									
Danger! Icebergs Ahead						x			
Hurricanes, Tornadoes and Blizzards						x			
In the Days of the Dinosaurs						x			
Rockets Into Space						x			
Rocks All Around Us						x			
Satellites in Outer Space						x			
Simple Machines and How They Work						x			
The Story of Chemistry						x			
The Story of Numbers						x			
The Story of the Atom						x			
Your Body and How It Works						x			
Your Wonderful World of Science						x			
Landmark Books									
American Into Orbit								x	x
Guadalcanal Diary								x	x
John F. Kennedy and PT-109								x	x
Lawrence of Arabia								x	x
The Story of Atomic Energy								x	x
The Story of D-Day								x	x
The Story of the Naval Academy								x	x
The Story of Scotland Yard								x	x
The War in Korea 1950–53								x	x
The West Point Story								x	x

HARPER & ROW, PUBLISHERS, 2500 Crawford Avenue, Evanston, Illinois 60201

	R	PP	P	1	2	3	4	5	6
American Adventure Series									
Portugee Phillips					x				
Friday the Arapaho Indian					x				
Squanto and the Pilgrims					x				
Pilot Jack Knight						x			
Alec Majors						x			
Chief Black Hawk						x			
Dan Morgan							x		
Cowboys and Cattle Trails							x		
Kit Carson							x		
Sabre Jet Ace								x	
Buffalo Bill								x	
Wild Bill Hickok								x	
Daniel Boone									x
Fur Trappers of the Old West									x
The Rush for Gold									x
John Paul Jones									x
Handbook on Corrective Reading (Betts)									

	R	PP	P	1	2	3	4	5	6
The Wonder Story Books									
Once Upon a Time				x					
I Know a Story				x					
It Happened One Day					x				
After the Sun Sets						x			
It Must Be Magic							x		
They Were Brave and Bold								x	
These Are the Tales They Tell									x

D. C. HEATH & CO., 1815 Prairie Avenue, Chicago, Illinois 60616

	R	PP	P	1	2	3	4	5	6
Our Animal Story Books									
Jumper the Deer				x					
The Little Crow				x					
Zeke the Raccoon				x					
Walt Disney Story Books									
Little Pig's Picnic and Other Stories				x	x				
Walt Disney's Bambi				x	x				
Teen Age Tales									
Teen Age Tales, Books A and B								x	x
Teen Age Tales, Books 1–6								x	x
It's Fun to Find Out Story Books									
Bus Driver						x	x		
The Mailman						x	x		
The Fireman						x	x		
The Food Store						x	x		
Tugboats						x	x		
Airport						x	x		
Farm Animals						x	x		

HOLT, RINEHART AND WINSTON, INC., 383 Madison Avenue, New York, New York 10017

	R	PP	P	1	2	3	4	5	6
Little Owl Reading Time Library									
Ten Pennies for Candy	x	x	x	x	x				
This Is My Family	x	x	x	x	x				
You Can Find a Snail	x	x	x	x	x				
Let's Take a Walk (36 other titles) (Guide)									

HOUGHTON-MIFFLIN, 1900 S. Batavia Ave., Geneva, Illinois 60134

	R	PP	P	1	2	3	4	5	6
Easy to Read Series									
The Cat in the Hat					x				
The Cat in the Hat Comes Back					x				
My Friend Mac					x				
Tiny Toosey's Birthday					x				
Vertle the Turtle					x				
Piper Books									
Kit Carson							x		
Christopher Columbus							x		
Amelia Earhart							x		

	R	PP	P	1	2	3	4	5	6
Benjamin Franklin							x		
Sam Houston							x		
Horace Mann							x		
Juan Ponce de Leon							x		
John Smith							x		
North Star Books									
Great Days of Whaling									x
Gold in California									x
Young Tom Edison									x
Sailing the Seven Seas									x
The Trail to Sante Fe								x	
Riders of the Pony Express								x	
Thoreau of Walden Pond								x	
Around the World with Nellie Bly									x
Indian Wars & Warriors—East									x
Indian Wars & Warriors—West									x
Donald McKay and the Clipper Ship								x	
Ticonderoga									x
Jenny Lind								x	
Lafayette in America									x
The Birth of Texas									x
Down the Colorado with Major Powell									x
Captured by the Mohawks									x
Washington Irving									x
The First Northwest Passage								x	
Robert E. Lee									x
Melville in the South Pacific									x
The Battle of Lake Erie									x

THE MACMILLAN CO., 434 S. Wabash Avenue, Chicago, Illinois 60605

	R	PP	P	1	2	3	4	5	6
Aviation Readers									
Straight Up				x					
Straight Down					x				
Core Vocabulary Readers									
The Ranch Book		x							
Macmillan Readers Unit Books									
Splash, Tuffy, and Boots at the Lake	x								
Snow, The Christmas Tree, Mr. & Mrs. Big		x							
Toby, Three Little Elephants, The Open Window				x					
Buster the Burro and three other titles					x				
Susan and the Sheet and three other titles						x			
Sports Readers									
Fun at the Playground					x				
Fun in Swimming						x			

G. P. PUTNAM AND SONS, 200 Madison Avenue, New York, New York

	R	PP	P	1	2	3	4	5	6
Horse in No Hurry							x		
Calvin and the Cub Scouts							x		

READER'S DIGEST SERVICES, INC., ED. DIVISION, Pleasantville, New York 10570

	R	PP	P	1	2	3	4	5	6
Pegasus Story Books									
Doc Stops a War					x	x			
Red Robin Fly Up					x	x			

BENJAMIN H. SANBORN & CO., L. W. Singer Co., 5601 N. W. Highway, Chicago, Ill. 60646

	R	PP	P	1	2	3	4	5	6
Famous Story Series									
The Story of Lemuel Gulliver									x
The Story of Robinson Crusoe									x
The Story of the Prince and the Pauper									x
The Story of the Three Musketeers									x
The Story of Treasure Island									x
The Story of Two Years Before the Mast									x
Sanborn Readers									
Fun For You				x					
Read Another Story					x	x			
Long, Long Ago						x	x		

SCOTT FORESMAN & CO., 433 E. Erie Street, Chicago 11, Illinois 60611

	R	PP	P	1	2	3	4	5	6
Special Reading Books									
Boxcar Children						x			
Mystery Ranch							x		
The Flying Trunk								x	
Adventures with Animals									x
Reading for Independence					x				
What Next Tall Tales						x			
Invitations to Personal Reading									
Big Talk				x					
The Sky Was Blue				x					
Rosa-Too-Little				x					
Karen's Opposites				x					
What Is a Turtle?				x					
(20 other titles) Teachers									
Book and Record Book				x					

CHARLES SCRIBNER'S SONS, 597 Fifth Ave., New York, New York 10017

	R	PP	P	1	2	3	4	5	6
Social Learnings Readers									
Bill's Story of the Wholesale Produce Market				x	x				
Bob's Story of the Retail Food Market				x	x				
Joe's Story of the Airport				x	x				

L. W. SINGER CO., INC. 249–259 West Erie Blvd., Syracuse, New York 13201

	R	PP	P	1	2	3	4	5	6
Carousel Books									
Hector, The Dog Who Loves Fleas				x					
My Daddy Lost His Job				x					

	R	PP	P	1	2	3	4	5	6
My Street				x					
(7 other titles)				x					

STECK-VAUGHN CO., Box 2028, Austin, Texas 78767

	R	PP	P	1	2	3	4	5	6
Easy Readers									
Dilly Dally	x	x	x	x	x				
Biffy	x	x	x	x	x				
Speedy Gets Around	x	x	x	x	x				
Where Is Cubby Bear?	x	x	x	x	x				
Rickie	x	x	x	x	x				
Willie Waddle	x	x	x	x	x				
Poke-Along	x	x	x	x	x				
Mouse Trail	x	x	x	x	x				
Pinkie	x	x	x	x	x				
Hoppy Long Legs	x	x	x	x	x				
The Sleepy Squirrel	x	x	x	x	x				
Up a Tree	x	x	x	x	x				
Boxes Are Wishes	x	x	x	x	x				
Carpy Cardinal	x	x	x	x	x				
Daffy	x	x	x	x	x				
The Elf Who Didn't Believe in Himself	x	x	x	x	x				
The Littlest Skunk	x	x	x	x	x				
Treasure Books									
Rip Van Winkle & Legend of Sleepy Hollow								x	
Kidnapped									x

WEBSTER DIVISION, McGraw-Hill Book Company, Manchester Rd., Manchester, Mo. 63011

	R	PP	P	1	2	3	4	5	6
Everyreader Series									
Cases of Sherlock Holmes							x		
Count of Monte Cristo							x		
Flamingo Feather							x		
The Gold Bug and Other Stories							x		
Ivanhoe							x		
Juarez, Hero of Mexico							x		
Man of Iron							x		
Simon Bolivar							x		
A Tale of Two Cities							x		
To Have and to Hold							x		
Junior Everyreader Series									
Bob, Son of Battle						x			
Indian Paint						x			
Jungle Trails						x			
King Arthur and His Knights						x			
Old Testament Stories						x			
The Robin Hood Stories						x			
The Trojan War						x			
Wild Animals I Have Known						x			
The Skyline Series									
Watch Out for C—Book A				x					

	R	PP	P	1	2	3	4	5	6
The Hidden Lookout—Book B						x			
Who Cares!—Book C							x		
Teacher's Guide for Series									

Trade Books

BERKELEY BOOKS, 145 West 57th Street, New York 19, New York

	R	PP	P	1	2	3	4	5	6
Boots and Saddles									x

THE JOHN DAY CO., 200 Madison Avenue, New York, New York 10016

	R	PP	P	1	2	3	4	5	6
The Reason Why Books									
Numerals						x	x	x	x
Why? A Book of Reasons						x	x	x	x

GOLDEN PRESS, INC., 850 Third Avenue, New York, New York 10022

	R	PP	P	1	2	3	4	5	6
Smokey Bear and the Campers					x				
Bambi									
Pinocchio									
Animals									
I Am a Boy									
A Dog's Life									
The Farm Book									
The Bug Book									
A Home for My Kittens									
A Dragon in a Wagon									

GROSSET AND DUNLAP, 1107 Broadway, New York, New York 10010

	R	PP	P	1	2	3	4	5	6
Bambi					x				

E. M. HALE AND CO., 1201 S. Hastings Way, Eau Claire, Wisconsin 54702

	R	PP	P	1	2	3	4	5	6
Blanco and the New World	x	x	x	x					
The Bunny Who Found Easter	x	x	x	x					
The Circus Baby	x	x	x	x					
Do You See What I See?	x	x	x	x					
Katy No-Pocket	x	x	x	x					
Ladybug, Ladybug!	x	x	x	x					
Mike's House	x	x	x	x					
Mittens	x	x	x	x					
The Runaway Bunny	x	x	x	x					
Shapes	x	x	x	x					
The Size of It and Ups and Downs	x	x	x	x					
The Tailor of Gloucester	x	x	x	x					
The Tale of Benjamin Bunny	x	x	x	x					
All Ready for Winter	x	x	x	x					
And to Think I Saw It on Mulberry Street			x	x	x				
Andy and the Lion			x	x	x				
Big Black Horse			x	x	x				
500 Hats of Bartholomew Cubbins			x	x	x				

	R	PP	P	1	2	3	4	5	6
Little Bruin and Par				x	x	x			
Little Indian Pottery Maker				x	x	x			
Little Toot				x	x	x			
Loopy				x	x	x			
Olaf Road				x	x	x			
Patrick Michael Kevin				x	x	x			
Snipp, Snapp, Snurr and the Gingerbread and the Big Surprise				x	x	x			
Wait for William				x	x	x			
Word Twins				x	x	x			
Billy and Blaze					x	x	x		
Coral Island					x	x	x		
Looking for Something					x	x	x		
Tammy Camps Out					x	x	x		
Tom's Magic TV					x	x	x		
Raggle-Taggle Fellow					x	x	x		
This Is Our Land					x	x	x		
Whistle Punk					x	x	x		
Galumph					x	x	x		
Hippolyte—Crab King					x	x	x		
Bobwhite From Egg to Chick to Egg						x	x	x	
The Five Chinese Brothers						x	x	x	
Jimmy's First Roundup						x	x	x	
How Baseball Began in Brooklyn						x	x	x	
Paul Bunyan Swings His Axe						x	x	x	
Space Ship Under the Apple Tree						x	x	x	
Terry Set Sail						x	x	x	
You Among the Stars						x	x	x	
How Big Is Big						x	x	x	
Little House on the Prairie							x	x	x
Pecos Bill and Lightning							x	x	x
Sleuth at Shortstop							x	x	x
Village That Learned to Read							x	x	x
Zorra								x	x	x
Digging into Yesterday								x	x	x
From Kite to Kittyhawk								x	x	x
Insect Builders and Craftsmen								x	x	x
Just So Stories								x	x	x
The Mystery Key								x	x	x
The Secret of Smugglers' Cove								x	x	x
Desert Dog									x	x
Mystery of the Black Diamonds									x	x
The 26 Letters									x	x

HARPER & ROW, PUBLISHERS, 2500 Crawford Avenue, Evanston, Illinois 60201

	R	PP	P	1	2	3	4	5	6
Noisy Book		x							
Red Tag Comes Back				x					
Little Chief				x					
Chester				x					
The Case of the Cat's Meow				x					
Here Comes Strikeout				x					
I Should Have Stayed in Bed				x	x				

	R	PP	P	1	2	3	4	5	6
The Case of the Hungry Stranger					x				
Railroad Engineers and Airplane Pilots					x				
Seeds and More Seeds					x				
Kick, Pass, and Run				x	x	x			
Jeannie's Hat				x	x	x			
The Case of the Dumb Bells				x	x	x			
Homework Caper				x	x	x			

ALFRED A. KNOPF, INC., 501 Madison Avenue, New York 22, New York

	R	PP	P	1	2	3	4	5	6
Made in Iceland										x

THE MACMILLAN COMPANY, 434 S. Wabash Avenue, Chicago, Illinois 60605

	R	PP	P	1	2	3	4	5	6
Reading Spectrum of Books									
Moving Day					x				
Six Foolish Fishermen					x				
Somebody's Pup					x				
Lucky and the Giant					x				
Taro and the Tofu						x			
A Hero by Mistake						x			
Crow Boy						x			
Pancho						x			
The Pile of Junk						x			
Baby Bears						x			
The Boy Who Got Mailed						x			
Dancing Cloud							x		
Bixxy and the Secret Message							x		
This Boy Cody							x		
Casey, the Utterly Impossible Horse							x		
Steve and the Burro's Secret							x		
The Blue-Nosed Witch							x		
Blaze Finds the Trail							x		
Big Horse, Little Horse							x		
Freddy							x		
The Lion, the Witch, and the Wardrobe							x	x	
The Pink Motel							x	x	
Told Under the Green Umbrella								x	
Little Major Leaguer								x	
The Spaceship Under the Apple Tree								x	
The Blonk from Beneath the Sea								x	
Call It Courage									x
The Reluctant Dragon									x
Thief Island									x
Grimm's Fairy Tales									x
Teacher's Guide									

PARENTS' MAGAZINE PRESS, INC., 52 Vanderbilt Avenue, New York, New York 10017

	R	PP	P	1	2	3	4	5	6
Tell Me a Riddle						x			
The Pony Express							x		
The Golden Spike							x		
The First Microscope								x	

	R	PP	P	1	2	3	4	5	6
REILLY AND LEE COMPANY, Chicago, Illinois									
The Littlest Star					x				

SCHOLASTIC BOOK SERVICES, 904 Sylvan Ave., Englewood Cliffs, N.J. 07632

	R	PP	P	1	2	3	4	5	6
Pivot Man									x
Book Clubs									
Map Skills Project Book One		x							
Map Skills Project Book Two					x	x			
Lucky Book Club									
Flip					x	x			
"I Can't," Said the Ant					x	x			
The Story of Ferdinand					x	x			
And 28 Other Titles					x	x			
Arrow Book Club									
The Superlative Horse							x	x	x
More Homer Price							x	x	x
Miss Pickerell Goes Undersea							x	x	x
United Nations							x	x	x
Birth of an Island							x	x	x
In the Days of the Dinosaurs							x	x	x
Wonders of the Human Body							x	x	x
Medals for Morse							x	x	x
Exploring Science in Your Home Laboratory							x	x	x
The Story of Helen Keller							x	x	x
Teen-Age Book Club									
Swiftwater									x
Eight Tales of Terror									x
Portrait of T. E. Lawrence									x
Campus Book Club									
The Story of the Second World War									x
Of Men and War									x
Home to India									x
Scholastic Literature Unit. "Courage."									
The Red Badge of Courage									x
The Sea Gulls Woke Me									x
Profiles in Courage (13 other titles)									x
Teacher's Guide & Student Notebook									

UNIVERSITY PUBLISHING CO., 1126 Que Street, Lincoln, Nebraska

	R	PP	P	1	2	3	4	5	6
Trail Riders					x	x			
Tales for a Tenderfoot							x	x	
Lujan Returns								x	x

WONDER BOOKS, INC., 1107 Broadway, New York 10, New York

	R	PP	P	1	2	3	4	5	6
The Giraffe Who Went to School					x				

APPENDIX G

Games, Activities, Audio-Visual Devices, and Teacher Resources

GAMES AND ACTIVITIES

THE GARRARD PRESS, 510 North Hickory Street, Champaign, Illinois 61820

Dolch Aids-To-Reading Materials	
Picture Readiness Game	Readiness
Who Gets It?	Readiness
Match, Set 1	Readiness
Match, Set 2	Readiness
Consonant Cards	Readiness
Vowel Cards	Readiness
Picture Word Cards	First
Popper Words, Set 1, Group Size	First
Popper Words, Set 1	First
Popper Words, Set 2	Second
Basic Sight Cards	Second
Sight Phrase Cards	Third
What The Letters Say	First
Consonant Lotto	First
Vowel Lotto	Second
Take	Third
Syllable Game	Third
Group Sounding Game	Third
Know Your States	Third
Read and Say Verb Game	Third

HARPER AND ROW, INC., 2500 Crawford Avenue, Evanston, Illinois 60201

Word-Go-Round (Teacher's Instructions)	Primary

IDEAL SCHOOL SUPPLY COMPANY, 8312–8346 Birkhoff Avenue, Chicago, Illinois 60620

Quiet Pal Game	Primary
The End-in-E Game	Primary
Rhyming Puzzle	Primary
Magic Cards Opposites	Primary
Magic Cards Consonant Blends	Primary
Magic Cards Initial Consonants	Primary
Magic Cards Vowels	Primary

THE JUDY COMPANY, 310 North 2nd Street, Minneapolis, Minnesota 55401

See-Quees
    Humpty Dumpty   Primary
    Gingerbread Boy   Primary

F. A. OWEN PUBLISHING COMPANY, Dansville, New York 14437

Picto-Word Flash Cards   Primary
Vowels and Vowel Digraphs (Charts and Cards)   Primary

FERON PUBLISHERS, 2165 Park Boulevard, Palo Alto, California 94306

The Remediation of Learning Disabilities
    (Handbook of Psychoeducational Resource Programs)   Elementary

SCOTT, FORESMAN AND COMPANY, 1900 East Lake, Glenview, Illinois 60025

Linguistic Block Series
    Rolling Phonics—Vowels (Teacher's Guide)   Primary
    Rolling Reader (Teacher's Guide)   Second

STECK-VAUGHN COMPANY, Box 16, Austin, Texas 78761

Reading Essentials Teaching Aids   First

AUDIO-VISUAL DEVICES

AUDIO TEACHING CENTER, 137 Hamilton Street, New Haven, Connecticut 06511

Voice-Master Tape Disc Programs
Spoken Arts Treasury of Fairy Tales
Imperial Tapes (pre-recorded in areas of readiness,
    study skills, comprehension skills, and word-attack
    skills)   Elementary

EDUCATIONAL DEVELOPMENTAL LABORATORIES, 824 Pulaski Road, Huntington, New York 11743

Controlled Reader
Controlled Reader Jr. (50 Watt)
Controlled Reader Filmstrips, Teacher's Manual, Stu-   Readiness–
    dent Books, and Tests   Secondary

Tach X Tachistoscope (500 Watt)
   Accuracy Building Discs   Readiness–
                                                 Grade 3
   Sight Vocabulary   Grades 1–3
   Spelling Lists   Grades 2–8

"Listen Look & Learn" Multi-Media Systems Approach
Uses new EDL and Aud X Audio-Visual unit, filmstrips, records, individual language arts activity
materials, and correlated reading library of Singer–
Random House books   Grades 1–3

ELECTRONIC FUTURES, INC., 57 Dodge Avenue, North Haven, Connecticut 06473

The EFI Reading Readiness Program   Grades K–2
The Audio Flashcard System
   (Reading, speech, number concepts, color discrimina-
   tion)   Grades K–8

ENCYCLOPAEDIA BRITANNICA EDUCATIONAL CORPORATION,
425 North Michigan Avenue, Chicago, Illinois 60611

Language Experiences in Reading Program   Elementary

THE MACMILLAN COMPANY, 434 South Wabash Avenue, Chicago,
Illinois 60605

Decoding For Reading
   Sixteen records
   Two Readalong Books for each child
   Teacher's Guide   Elementary

RHEEM CALIFONE, Dept. R 68, Los Angeles, California 90016

Rheem Califone Reading Programs
   Uses teacher and student manuals and programmed   Elementary–
   tapes for all phases of remedial reading programs   Secondary

SCIENCE RESEARCH ASSOCIATES, 259 East Erie Street, Chicago, Illinois 60611

OPTA Overhead Projector Tachistoscopic Adaptor

SCOTT, FORESMAN AND COMPANY, 1900 East Lake, Glenview, Illinois
60025

Vocabulary Development Program Volumes I and II   Elementary

TWEEDY TRANSPARENCIES, 207 Hollywood Avenue, East Orange, New Jersey 07018

Tweedy Visual-Lingual Reading Program	
Consists of 48 transparencies and teacher's manual	Primary

TEACHER RESOURCES

GINN AND COMPANY, 450 W. Algonquin Road, Arlington Heights, Illinois 60005

V Is for Verse	Teacher
Let's Listen (3 auditory training records and manual)	Primary
Let's Play a Game	Primary
Reading Activities for Middle Grades	Intermediate
Help Yourself to Read, Write, and Spell	Fourth–Sixth

THE GARRARD PRESS, 510 North Hickory Street, Champaign, Illinois 61820

Games and Stunts to Read and Play, Set 1, Book 1	Primary
Read and Play, Set 1, Books 2 and 3	Primary
Read and Play, Set 2, Books 1, 2, 3	Primary

IMPERIAL PRODUCTIONS, INC., Kankakee, Illinois 60901

Primary Reading Program (Taped) Lesson 10 Sample	Primary

PACIFIC PRODUCTIONS, INC., 414 Mason Street, San Francisco, California 94102

Filmstrip Reading Series	
Structural Analysis (2)	Elementary
Using Books Efficiently (2)	Junior High
Reading for Understanding (2)	Senior High
Learning to Use the Dictionary (2)	
Phonetic Analysis (4)	

SCOTT, FORESMAN & COMPANY, 1900 East Lake, Glenview, Illinois 60025

Filmstrips for Practice in Phonetic Skills	
Rhyme Time—Beginning Sounds—Letters and Sounds	Primary
Fun with Words	Primary

Sounds Around Us (3 Auditory Training Records)	
Around the House, the Farm, the Town	Primary

Index